Vietnamese Classifiers in Narrative Texts

Summer Institute of Linguistics and
The University of Texas at Arlington
Publications in Linguistics

Publication 125

Publications in Linguistics is a series published jointly by the Summer Institute of linguistics and the University of Texas at Arlington. The series is a venue for works covering a broad range of topics in linguistics, but primarily the analytical treatment of minority languages from all parts of the world. While most volumes are authored by members of the Institute, suitable works by others also form part of the series.

Series Editors

Mildred L. Larson, Summer Institute of Linguistics
Donald A Burquest, University of Texas at Arlington

Volume Editors

Marilyn A Mayers
Bonnie Brown

Production Staff

Laurie Nelson, Production Manager, Compositor
Hazel Shorey, Graphic Arts

Vietnamese Classifiers in Narrative Texts

Karen Ann Daley

A Publication of
The Summer Institute of Linguistics
and
The University of Texas at Arlington
1998

©1998 by the Summer Institute of Linguistics, Inc.
Library of Congress Catalog No: 97-61945
ISBN: 1-55671-021-6
ISSN: 1040-0850

Printed in the United States of America
All Rights Reserved

08 07 06 05 04 03 02 01 00 99   10 9 8 7 6 5 4 3 2 1

No part of this publication may be reproduced, stored in a retrieval system, or transmitted in any form or by any means—electronic, mechanical, photocopy, recording, or otherwise—without the express permission of the Summer Institute of Linguistics, with the exception of brief excerpts in journal articles or reviews.

The four Vietnamese narrative texts presented in appendix B in technical format originally appeared in *Once in Vietnam: The Bridge of Reunion and Other Stories* and *Once in Vietnam: A Shadow on the Wall and Other Stories* and are used by permission of National Textbook Company, Lincolnwood, Ill.

Copies of this and other publications of the Summer Institute of Linguistics may be obtained from

International Academic Bookstore
7500 W Camp Wisdom Road
Dallas, TX 75236

Voice: 972-708-7404
Fax: 972-708-7433
E-mail: academic_books@sil.org
Internet: http://www.sil.org

Contents

Abbreviations ix

Preface xi

1. Introduction 1
   1.1. The problem 2

          1.2–1.3 Theoretical framework for this study

   1.2. Discourse functions attributed to classifiers 3
   1.3. The lexical set classifier as defined by Thompson 5
   1.4. Hypotheses examined in this study 9
   1.5. Scope of the study 9

          1.6–1.7 Definition of terms

   1.6. Classifier types 11
   1.7. Discourse functions 11

2. Literature Review 15
   2.1. General overview 15
   2.2. Numeral classifiers in Vietnamese 17
   2.3. Classifiers in discourse 19
   2.4. Previous discourse studies on Vietnamese 20
   2.5. Summary 21

3. Methodology 23
   3.1. The corpus 24

                   3.2–3.5 Methodology

   3.2. Data preparation and coding 28
   3.3. Quantitative distribution analysis 35
   3.4. Discourse analysis of reference 40
   3.5. Cross-linguistic comparison 47

4. Results 49

                    4.1–4.3 Numbers

   4.1. Prototypical numeral classifier constructions 50
   4.2. The significance of higher and lower numbers
       in the data 52
   4.3. Numbers functioning as non-numbers 55

                  4.4–4.6 Definiteness

   4.4. Definiteness and indefiniteness 56
   4.5. Classifiers as markers of initial mentions 60
   4.6. Classifiers and anaphoric reference 61

        4.7–4.8 Distribution of classifiers compared
             to other strategies of referring

   4.7. Strategies of referring in Vietnamese 64
   4.8. Distribution of classifiers with regard to
       referent continuity 65

      4.9–4.10 Referent importance and referent continuity

   4.9. Overall frequency 71
   4.10. Referential distance and referential persistence 73

    4.11–4.12 Cross-linguistic comparison of classifier functions

   4.11. Anaphoric use of classifiers in Japanese compared
       to Vietnamese 78
   4.12. Referential salience in White Hmong compared
       to Vietnamese 80

        4.13–4.18 Additional considerations

   4.13. Individuation 88
   4.14. Abstractness 90
   4.15. Relativization 90

Contents

    4.16. Marking possession and classifiers. 90
    4.17. Nominalization 93
    4.18. Kin term or classifier? 95

5. Conclusion 101
    5.1. Summary of findings. 101
    5.2. Modifying classifiers, general categoricals, and
         kin classifiers 103
    5.3. The advantages of discourse-based analysis. 104

         5.4–5.6 Implications of the study

    5.4. Grammaticalization of classifiers 104
    5.5. Numeral or nominal?. 106
    5.6. Are all nouns classifiable? 107

         5.7–5.9 Directions for further research

    5.7. Subtypes of classifiers 108
    5.8. Classifiers and thematic continuity 108
    5.9. Classifier use in other discourse genres 109

Appendix A. List of Classifiers in the Data and Additional
    Tables. 111

Appendix B. Four Vietnamese Narrative Texts. 119
    Key to the interlinearized texts 119
    A Broken Sword 120
    Mission Impossible. 144
    Son Tinh and Thuy Tinh 161
    The Story of the Mosquito 183

References. 203

Abbreviations

Brackets are used in the grammatical tags and free translation fields to indicate: (1) conventional grammatical categories which differ from the categories listed in the reference grammar used for this study, (2) lexical items whose grammatical category changes from context to context, and (3) lexical items which function like a member of the tagged category, but which are not identified as members of the category in the reference grammar used for this study (Thompson 1965). The symbol [<] indicates that the corresponding morpheme forms a compound with the preceding morpheme.

ABB	abbreviation
AGM	agentive marker
AJ	adjective
AUX	auxiliary
AV	adverb
ASP	aspect
CAT	category
CJ	conjunction
CL	classifier
CP	copulative verb
DM	demonstrative
FW	function word
GC	general categorical
IDN	indefinite noun (e.g., any)

INT	interrogative
ITJ	interjection
KCL	kin classifier
KIN	kinship term
[lit]	literary
MC	modifying classifier
MD	modal
N	noun
NAM	proper name
NEG	negative
NG	negative
NP	noun phrase
NU	numeral, number
OF	overall frequency
PASS	passive
PL	pluralizer
PRE	preposition
PRO	pronoun
PRT	particle
QNF	quantifier
QW	question word
RD	referential difference
RN	relator noun (similar to a preposition in English)
RP	referential persistence
SV	stative verb
V	verb
1s	first person, singular
1p	first person, plural
3s	third person, singular
3p	third person, plural
1s^SUP	first person, singular, status or attitude of speaker is superior
3s^ARROG	third person, singular; speaker considers the referent arrogant

Preface

Classifiers in Vietnamese are said to have numerous syntactic and semantic functions, including nominalization, individuation, anaphoric reference, and marking definiteness or possession. However, unclassified NPs may also have some of these functions, and few classified NPs conform to the so-called prototypical classifier construction for Vietnamese. Consequently, the reason a speaker chooses to use a classifier is not apparent. In this investigation, perhaps the first discourse study of classifiers in Vietnamese to date, the distribution of classifiers in four narratives is analyzed, using text-based measurements (referential accessibility, referential distance, referential persistence, overall frequency; Givón 1983), and four criteria from a study of classifiers in White Hmong (Riddle 1989). The findings indicate referential salience is the basic discourse function for classifiers in Vietnamese.

This study is adapted from my thesis done as partial fulfillment of the requirements for my master of arts degree from the University of Texas at Arlington. I was privileged to have had Dr. Herring direct me in this work. I appreciate the valuable feedback I received from Drs. Silva and Paolillo, and I thank all of these professors for sharing their expertise with young linguists like me. I also thank Mimi Barker for her attentive and generous assistance, and day-to-day camaraderie. Although I relied heavily upon her and others for their knowledge of Vietnamese, the mistakes are mine alone.

I thank Karen White Wells for her patience and willingness to share her expertise in computers, and for assisting me in the preparation and printing of my thesis.

I would like to thank Graham Hawks of the National Textbook Company for granting me permission to use four of their Vietnamese narratives in this study (and to reprint them here).

I offer special thanks to my parents, who have amazed me by always assuming I had the ability to accomplish high academic goals. I am especially thankful for my husband, Steve, without whose help and encouragement I would not have completed this project

Most of all, I am grateful to our Creator, who made language truly beautiful, and who gave me the heart and mind to revel in it.

1
Introduction

A CLASSIFIER is a function word that occurs with and categorizes a noun or verb or another classifier. The two most common types of classifiers are numeral and nominal. In numeral classifier systems, the principal semantic function of the classifier is quantification, which includes both multiplicity and individuation (Greenberg 1977; Allan 1977; Craig 1994). In languages with such systems, of which Vietnamese is one, a NP which contains a number or quantifier normally also contains a classified noun. The classifier in a numerated NP categorizes the noun on the basis of the measure or sort of thing counted, e.g., 'three bags (of) rice', in which the word for 'bag' is the classifier. A classifier in a nominal system is used to describe a noun in terms of some sense of the noun itself: a physical attribute such as shape or substance, e.g., *pencil* (literally, 'flat object pencil'), in which the word for pencil is categorizied by the classifier referring to flat or oblong objects; or a human relationship, e.g., *younger brother* (literally, 'child younger sibling boy'), in which the word for child is the classifier. From a typological perspective, a language which employs one or both types of function words is considered a classifier language.

Until recently, studies of classifier systems have concentrated on the syntactic and lexico-semantic aspects of classifier usage. More recently, anaphoric reference has also been recognized as a classifier function in several numeral classifier languages (Burmese, Jacaltec, Japanese, Thai, Vietnamese). However, few analysts have explored the anaphoric function of classifiers in depth. (Some exceptions are: Becker 1986; Craig

1986; Denny 1986; Downing 1986; Hopper 1986; Riddle 1989.) This line of research crucially involves considering the use of classifiers in discourse.

Discourse-based study of classifiers holds promise as a means of explaining their distribution in actual use. Indeed, the linguists investigating the discourse functions of classifiers have discovered classifiers functioning as more than just anaphoric referents. For example, classified NPs in Japanese, Malay, and Burmese frequently mark the introduction of a new topic in discourse. In Yao languages, classifiers may affect the definiteness and topicality of their NPs. Classifiers in Japanese mark the status of referents in a way that other anaphoric devices cannot. For instance, human classifiers (e.g., *nin* 'human being') in Japanese provide speakers with an attitudinally neutral option for human anaphoric reference, in contrast with other Japanese anaphoric forms.

The systematic discourse functions of classifiers mentioned above suggest that it may be necessary to look beyond the lexical or phrase level to resolve structural and functional inconsistencies associated with classifier use. Consequently, study of classifiers in the larger discourse context is a logical step toward better understanding classifier systems.

In this chapter I present a description of classifiers with a brief explanation of the Vietnamese classifier system, a statement of the problem, the theoretical framework for the study, my hypotheses, and definitions of key terms. Chapters 2 and 3 contain a review of the relevant literature on classifiers and a description of the discourse-based methodology applied in this study, respectively. In chapter 4, a summary of the findings and a detailed description of the analysis are given. In chapter 5, I conclude with some implications of the present study concerning classifier languages in general and Vietnamese in particular, and propose recommendations for future research.

Appendix A contains the list of classifiers found in the data and statistics which are summarized in chapter 4. Appendix B contains the four texts used in this study, complete with morpheme-by-morpheme glosses, grammatical tags, and free translations. Each text is preceded by a plot summary in English.

1.1. The problem. Vietnamese is an Austroasiatic language whose classifier inventory numbers over a hundred, although exact counts are generally not given. Classifiers in Vietnamese perform an array of syntactic and semantic functions, from nominalization, individuation, occurrence with a noun which is modified by a relative clause, marking possession or definiteness, to substituting for nouns. The problem with such a list, however, is that in actual use, both classified and nonclassified NPs can be found fulfilling each syntactic and semantic function. Sometimes classifiers appear in nominalized forms, and sometimes they do not; sometimes they appear with relative clauses, and sometimes not; sometimes they mark possession, and sometimes possession is marked without classifiers; and so on. The question then arises: Is there a unifying criterion which guides a speaker's choice in any given instance to use a classifier or not?

In this investigation, I analyze classifier use in four written narrative texts in Vietnamese. I argue that referential salience is the single discourse-level function that can explain the diversity of uses attributed to classifiers in Vietnamese. In Vietnamese discourse, a speaker uses classifiers to highlight salient referents. I also illustrate how a discourse-based investigation of numeral classifier systems answers questions that studies based solely on syntactic structure and lexico-semantics cannot accurately answer.

1.2–1.3 Theoretical framework for this study

1.2. Discourse functions attributed to classifiers. In numeral and nominal classifier systems, the use of classifiers pertains to nominal reference. That is, a classifier construction is one of many referring strategies, among which are pronouns, proper nouns, zero anaphora, and unclassified nouns. The reason why a particular reference form is used in a given syntactic environment is best understood in terms of discourse relations. For example, the status of information as new or given (old) is a discourse relation that affects the use of proper nouns versus pronouns. The proper noun in (1a), establishes *Josephine* as a new referent, or new information. Once introduced, Josephine is a given and can be referred to by using the pronoun *she* in (1b). Likewise, the clause in (1a) *gave birth...and has been sleeping...*is referred to as given information by the use of the demonstrative pronoun *that* in (1b).

(1)   a. Josephine gave birth to an 11-pound boy at three this morning and has been sleeping ever since.
         b. She had been in labor for seventeen hours before that.

The way discourse relations such as given and new information affect anaphoric functions such as pronominal reference are not apparent in smaller syntactic contexts. Anaphoric function is just one of the properties of classifiers that implies discourse relations. Another discourse function that has been attributed to classifiers is marking definiteness. Like the anaphoric relationship between a reference form and its antecedent, the definiteness of a NP is determined by factors related to discourse structure. In example (2), I have removed the definiteness marker from the mention of *family*. To name only a few possibilities, the NP with the missing marker could refer to 'the family', 'a family', 'my family', or 'their family'.

(2) In the early 1900s, much of the property had been cleared of all marketable timber. Then ___ **family** became interested in the apples from the trees the loggers overlooked and purchased the land. (Kelly and Kelly 1993)

If readers were to choose an appropriate marker for definiteness of the missing form in (2), they could do so only with regard to the larger discourse environment. By examining the environment immediately preceding the missing form in (2), reproduced in (3), the reader can gather more information about *family*. For example, by reading (3), one can determine that family has not been mentioned in the immediately preceding environment. Consequently, the missing form in (2) may be a newly introduced referent and could be indefinite. However, it is also possible that family had been introduced much earlier in the discourse (for example, in the preface or in the chapter preceding the chapter of the current mention), in which case the referent in question could be definite.

(3) Quaker Center, Ben Lomond, CA

At the end of a steep and winding country road a mile up from Ben Lomond, the Quaker Center occupies 80 acres on the slopes of the Santa Cruz Mountains. It sits high among the redwoods and fir trees, where coastal fog drifts in to give needed moisture to the forest. (Kelly and Kelly 1993)

Like the preceding environment, the environment immediately succeeding (2), shown in (4), also provides more information. However, the small succeeding environment still leaves the question of the definiteness of family in (2) ambiguous. The amount of context I have provided for this example is insufficient to accurately determine the definiteness of the NP in (2). From this example we see that definiteness, along with many other facets of nominal reference, are understood precisely only in terms of the larger discourse environment.

Introduction 5

(4) They hosted scouting groups in the 1940s and later on groups concerned with preserving the environment. (Kelly and Kelly 1993)

The example in (2) represents a hypothetical situation since a writer would not withhold a particular word in actual communication, as was done here. However, the example is especially relevant for analysts who are concerned with accurately assessing grammatical relationships in synthetic languages such as Vietnamese, which exhibit little syntactic marking at the word, phrase, and clause levels. In these kinds of languages, the analyst can learn much about a language's structure by observing the distribution of particular constituents in discourse.

Discourse analysis allows the analyst to consider the functions of a constituent (in this instance, classifiers) in an environment which is large enough to show both the conditions under which the constituent appears, as well as the conditions under which it is absent. Using textual data, one can isolate particular properties of the textual environment and of specific constituents. By isolating and examining characteristics of the classifier constructions in text, one can then compare the discourse functions of classifiers with their syntactic and semantic functions.

1.3. The lexical set classifier as defined by Thompson. In order to begin analyzing the classifiers in Vietnamese, it is necessary to identify which words belong to the lexical set CLASSIFIER. In this section I describe the structural parameters for the lexical sets CLASSIFIER and GENERAL CATEGORICAL from Thompson (1965), a commonly-cited Vietnamese reference grammar. By Thompson's definitions, these two lexical sets are subtypes of classifiers, and the hypernym applying to both sets is CATEGORICAL. However, for this research, I refer to Thompson's subtype classifier as MODIFYING CLASSIFIER while retaining the name GENERAL CATEGORICAL for the other subtype. This allows me to reserve the term CLASSIFIER for the general term applying to both sets.

As a background for understanding the terms modifying classifier and general categorical, it is necessary to examine briefly the notion of constituent structure as described by Thompson (1965). In Thompson's terminology, a CONSTITUTE is a sequence of constituents which can be separated into two or more parts. Those parts "balance one another in the makeup of the whole" (1965:110). Every constitute may be subdivided into smaller constitutes "until the level of single morphemes is reached and no further divisions can be made" (1965:110). Within a given constitute, when a longer constituent can be substituted for a shorter constituent while bearing the same relationship to the immediate constituents as the shorter one, it is called an EXPANSION. The shorter constituent is called the MODEL. For example, in (5), *Karen's committee chair* is an expansion for the model *Susan*.

(5) a. **Karen's committee chair** sings in the shower.
    b. **Susan** sings in the shower.

When one of the immediate constituents of a constitute is the model of the constitute itself in a larger context, it is called a NUCLEAR MODEL. Example (6) illustrates this concept, where the constitute is the first sentence in a story. The constitute (6a), which is the opening sentence of the narrative, can be replaced by the nuclear model (6b).

(6) a. *Ng y xưa có người hiếu-lợi, một hôm ra chợ, gặp ng y chợ phi n vừa đông người đến buôn b n vừa lắm đồ h ng.*
    Once upon a time there was a greedy person who one day went out into the market place on a day of a fair when there were both a great many people who had come to do business and a great deal of merchandise.

    b. *Ng y xưa có người hiếu-lợi.*
    Once upon a time there was a greedy person. (Thompson 1965:112)

In Thompson's terminology, a nuclear model of either another nuclear model or a complete sentence is the HEAD (1965:114). Conversely, that constituent in a constitute which is not the head is the COMPLEMENT (1965:114). Both DESCRIPTIVE and RESTRICTIVE complements are defined by syntactic structure: in Vietnamese, a descriptive complement follows the head, and a restrictive complement precedes the head (1965:125).

With the aforementioned grammatical categories in mind, Thompson (1965:193) defines modifying classifiers as follows:

> [They] do not occur as single-word descriptive complements. They are most common as heads in descriptive phrases... [and] have an important class meaning: while they usually refer to rather general categories of objects or concepts, they are specific in identifying single, individual units; without a preceding number to specify a given quantity the meaning is clearly one unit.

Introduction

As head of a descriptive phrase,[1] a modifying classifier (MC) can categorize either a nominal or verbal concept. While a noun denotes the referent itself, a MC describes the referent as a unit of the semantic set denoted by the noun. A verb denotes the action itself, and a MC denotes the action as a nominal concept. Examples (7) and (8) show an instance of each usage. In example (7), the MC *con* 'animal' classifies the noun *trâu* 'buffalo' in the descriptive phrase 'three male buffaloes'. In (8) and (9), the MCs *cuộc* and *sự* both classify verbs. The MC *cuộc* normally classifies some sort of interaction, and the MC *sự* normally classifies events (Thompson 1965:195).

(7) Mission:10[2]

người	hãy	đem	ba	con	trâu	đực
person	beˆsureˆto	take	three	animal	buffalo	male
GC	[MD]	V	NU	MC	N	[AJ]

Take three male buffaloes

(8) Mosquito:8[3]

n ng	không	ưa	cuộc	sống	nghèo	n n
damsel	not	like	[interaction]	beˆalive	destitute	<
KCL	NG	V	MC	[SV]	[AJ]	

She did not like her poor life

(9) Mosquito:37

không	chống	trả	nổi	sự	c m	dỗ
not	oppose	giveˆback	beˆableˆto	[event]	seduce	coax
NG	V	V	[SV]	[MC]	V	V

mãnh	liệt	đó
fierce	violent	that
[AJ]	[AJ]	DM

Not able to resist such provocative promises

---

[1] Thompson uses the term phrase in its conventional sense.

[2] All the Vietnamese texts are written in standard Vietnamese orthography; each example is preceded by the name I have assigned to the text and the sentence number.

[3] The symbol [<] indicates that the corresponding morpheme forms a compound with the preceding morpheme.

General categoricals, like MCs, appear as the heads of descriptive phrases. Unlike MCs, however, they do occur as single-word descriptive complements (Thompson 1965:192). In other words, general categoricals (GC) may be used pronominally, but MCs may not. Both MCs and GCs "refer to entities as members of general classes rather than as specifically characterized concepts" (Thompson 1965:197). The GC *người* 'person' is shown as a single-word descriptive complement in (7) and as the head of a descriptive complement in (10).

(10) Mission:4

> *người   nông   dân   ngạc   nhi n*
> person farmer citizen choke   so
> GC   N   N   V   [CJ]
> The peasant was puzzled

Thompson's categories are determined on the basis of syntax, and in isolation—that is, at the sentence level or smaller—the structural parameters of the two classifier subtypes neatly describe them. However, when the classifier NPs in the larger discourse context are looked at closely, the syntactic parameters cease to keep the subtypes distinct. In discourse, both classifier types may be used in the same environments and with the same syntactic patterns. The reason for this, I propose, lies in their discourse functions and not solely in their structural description. Thus, I begin this study by distinguishing between the syntactic categories modifying classifier and general categorical, but set aside the distinction between these subtypes of classifiers when discourse functions override them.

1.4. Hypotheses examined in this study. A prototypical pattern, by definition, is the standard after which other forms are modeled. It is often, but not necessarily, the most frequently encountered of all forms of a similar type. Any given numeral classifier language has a prototypical numeral classifier construction. According to some analysts, in Vietnamese the prototypical syntactic pattern for classifier use is number + classifier + noun. With regard to this pattern, I first hypothesize that, contrary to an alleged typological universal for numeral classifier languages, a classifier is not obligatory in numeral phrases in Vietnamese. In other words, this single syntactic requirement is not the basis for classifier use.

Second, several functions attributed to classifiers in Vietnamese imply discourse level relations (particularly anaphoric reference), but the

Introduction   9

prototypical syntactic pattern is a phrase level construction. Therefore, I hypothesize that in discourse, many classifier constructions in Vietnamese do not conform to the prototypical syntactic pattern.

Third, I compare the discourse use of classifiers in two other languages with the use of classifiers in Vietnamese. I examine the Vietnamese data for evidence of classifier discourse functions known to exist in Japanese and White Hmong. In Japanese, classifiers are used anaphorically (Downing 1986), and in White Hmong, classifiers are used to increase referential salience (Riddle 1989; Adams 1991). Both Japanese and White Hmong are from language families which are genetically unrelated to Vietnamese;[4] however, White Hmong and Vietnamese share geographic proximity as well as areal features with other languages of the Sino-Tibetan, Tai, and Austroasiatic families.[5] Because of their linguistic similarities, I hypothesize that the Vietnamese and White Hmong classifier systems will prove to be more similar than the Japanese and Vietnamese systems.

Fourth, I hypothesize that the discourse function of referential salience (the same function of classifiers in White Hmong) will account for the disparate syntactic, semantic, and discursive functions that have been attributed to classifiers in Vietnamese.

1.5. Scope of the study. In terms of modality, I exclude considerations of spoken discourse from this research because my data are written materials. Furthermore, because these written materials are narratives, I do not presume that the conclusions drawn from this study necessarily generalize to expository, hortatory, or other discourse types. As a particular type of narrative (folk tales), the materials evidence some linguistic features which are characteristic of and perhaps unique to a specific genre of narrative. However, since folk tales are prototypical narratives in many cultures, including Vietnamese, many of the observations from this study are also likely to enlighten our understanding of narratives as a general discourse type. Another fact about the texts that limits the scope of generalization possible from this research is their intended audience. These tales are traditional stories that have been told for hundreds of years from generation to generation of Vietnamese people; however, these particular texts were written for

---

[4]Vietnamese is an Austroasiatic language (Nguyễn Đinh Hoa in Comrie 1987). The language classification of White Hmong is controversial; White Hmong is tentatively considered to be in the Sino-Tibetan family (DeLancey in Comrie 1987; Crystal 1992). Japanese is an isolate (Crystal 1992).

[5]Vietnamese and White Hmong share the same SVO word order, both are tonal and isolating, and their words are primarily monosyllabic (Purnell 1962; Nguyễn Đinh Hoa in Comrie 1987).

bilingual (Vietnamese and English) readers around the age of twelve (Trần Van Điền and Trần Cảnh Xuân 1993; Barker p.c.). Consequently, the texts exhibit the level of linguistic complexity and intellectual challenge appropriate to that audience.

While I base one of the hypotheses for this research on a study of classifiers in Japanese, I do not base the methodology for this study on it. For example, I do not compare referent striking distances, which indicate the related feature referential accessibility. The striking distance, that is, the number of intervening clause boundaries, sentence boundaries, and mentions of other referents between the antecedent and the anaphor in question, is used to compare the placement of classifiers, ellipses, pronouns, and nouns in terms of referent identifiability (Downing 1986:357–62). In omitting the striking distance tabulations, I ignore the relative levels of referential accessibility associated with anaphoric classifiers compared with other anaphoric reference forms. However, I do account for the referential accessibility of referents using Givón's REFERENTIAL ACCESSIBILITY (RA) measurement as well as by applying criteria from a study of White Hmong; see   3.2 and 4.11–4.12.

In terms of specific types of classifiers, I treat time measurement classifiers and kin classifiers differently from the other classifiers in the data. Even though they frequently contain classifiers, time expressions in Vietnamese are normally idiomatic expressions which state collateral, rather than thematic information. For example, the phrase 'once upon a time' (11) is literally glossed as 'a long time ago day'. Expressions like this one were not included in any of the statistics for noun phrases.

(11)   ng y   xưa
       day   a^long^time^ago
       MC   [AJ]
       once upon a time

In relation to the overall discourse, time expressions often consist of background or setting information, so study of them should be assessed in terms of comparable phenomena. This study focuses on the discourse function of classifiers with regard to referential strategies; consequently, classifiers in time expressions fall outside of its scope.

An area I address in a rudimentary way is the use of kin classifiers. Unlike other classifiers, kin classifiers categorize on the basis of social hierarchy or aspects of human relationships (Adams 1986:246). Thus, the use of kin classifiers involves not only the dynamics of the classifier system, but also the dynamics of the kinship system. Since my study addresses just one of those dynamics, the classifier subtype kin invites a more complete study in the future.

Finally, the study is done on a small scale. The data consist of four narratives of eight hundred or fewer words each. For the sake of generalization, it is assumed that specific textual features that function a certain way throughout these four texts will exhibit the same tendencies throughout larger samples of discourse of a similar genre. Regardless of whether or not subsequent investigations bear out this generalization, the present investigation is among the first steps taken toward filling the void in the literature with regard to discourse-based analysis of Vietnamese. It is hoped that the results will shed light on the functions of classifiers in Vietnamese.

1.6–1.7 Definition of terms

This section contains definitions of key terms used in the study. The terms are arranged in two sets: classifier types, and discourse functions. Within each set of definitions, the terms are arranged in alphabetical order.

1.6. Classifier types. A CLASSIFIER is a function word that is used with a noun, a verb, or another classifier to categorize the referent on the basis of a single attribute. A classifier may categorize a referent with regard to dimension, shape, or other physical characteristic (such as round); human or social relationship (such as elder sibling or respected); or the sort or amount of the referent being talked about (such as droplet).

GENERAL CATEGORICALS and MODIFYING CLASSIFIERS are subtypes of classifiers in Vietnamese and have already been discussed in 1.3.

For the purposes of this study, the kin terms that can be used as classifiers are counted in the data as KIN CLASSIFIERS. Guidelines for identifying kin classifiers are primarily semantic in nature; however, their distribution in text suggests that this is a valid grammatical subcategory. For discussion of kin classifiers, see 4.6 and 4.18.

1.7. Discourse functions. ANAPHORIC REFERENCE denotes a grammatical form which takes its interpretation from some other part of the discourse. For example, in the sentence 'Galina dressed Igmar's wound so he would heal properly', 'he' is an anaphoric reference which refers to 'Igmar'. Anaphoric reference is sometimes used to describe backwards reference exclusively (as opposed to cataphoric or forward reference). As the comparison between forward and backward reference is not relevant in this study, the term is used to denote the grammatical relationship of co-reference in general.

ZERO ANAPHORA is a type of anaphoric reference whereby an entity is referred to but not explicitly mentioned. A clause contains a zero anaphor or elliptical mention when the NP filling a particular case role is required by the verb (or preposition), but is not present as an explicit referent (Clancy 1980; Downing 1986).[6] (As a case in point, in the preceding subordinate clause 'but is not...referent', the entity referred to is a zero anaphor representing 'the NP filling a particular case role' in the previous clause.)

When a speaker is talking about a referential entity and believes that the hearer can identify the same entity, the speaker syntactically codes the NP as DEFINITE. The hearer may identify the referent based on clues from the deictic situation, prior cultural knowledge, or information that has been presented earlier in the discourse (Givón 1990:922–24). This study is concerned with definiteness as it is expressed in the grammar of discourse. For an example of a NP coded as definite and its relationship to discourse, see 1.2.

DISCONTINUOUS REFERENT denotes an NP which is a newly introduced or reintroduced referent. When a referent is being reintroduced, at least one different referent has been mentioned in the same pragmatic case role (i.e., the subject or object of a simple clause) since the most recent previous mention of the currently reintroduced referent. CONTINUOUS REFERENT refers to a NP in the current clause which was present in the preceding clause in the same pragmatic case role. Characteristically, a continuous referent that is also important thematically will continue to appear in the same case role in succeeding clauses.

Because the grammatical functions of words in Vietnamese are remarkably malleable,[7] I do not define referent by the popular criterion applied to a noun phrase proper, that is, by the notion that the head of a

---

[6]In Vietnamese, the distinction between a verb and a preposition is sometimes ambiguous. Some linguists have analyzed a middle category between the two parts of speech using the term coverbs (e.g., Clark 1978).

[7]Languages of the southeast Asian linguistic area present the analyst with a categorization problem in terms of syntactic and semantic categories. Some grammarians create their own terminology in "despair of imposing ready-made 'Standard Average European' category-labels on all form-classes and construction types" (Matisoff 1991:445). While it is difficult to distinguish and name many grammatical categories found in Vietnamese, in most cases I use conventional terms which most nearly fit the function of the word in question.

noun phrase can only be a noun which is indicated as such in a prescriptive, published lexicon.⁸ Rather, for the term referent I adopt the meaning used in Du Bois (1980:208): "A noun phrase is (a referent) when it is used to speak about an object as an object, with continuous identity over time." In the definition of referent, 'object' may refer to a physical object or concept, real or hypothetical. In example (12), the noun phrases 'a pagoda', 'a high mountain', 'a young man [who] had been raised by a Buddhist monk', '[the] Buddhist monk', 'him', and 'martial arts' are referents. In (13) the phrase 'the point of the young man's sword' is a referent, as well as 'the extremely strong-handed stabbing', even though the head of the latter expression đâm 'stab' is a verb rather than a noun.

(12) Sword:9, 10

có	ch ng	thanh ni n	được	một	nh
exist	young^man	youth <	[PASSIVE]	one/a	respected
V	KCL	N> <	ASP	NU	CAT

sư	nuôi	dường	ở	một	ngôi
Buddhist^monk	rear	support	be^located^at	one/a	temple
N	V	V	[SV]	NU	[CL]

chùa	tr n	núi	cao.	H ng ng y	nh
temple	on/upon	mountain	be^high	daily <	respected
N	RN	N	SV	[N] CAT	[CAT]

sư	dạy	cậu c c	môn	võ thuật.
Buddhist^monk	teach	3s various	martial^arts <	<
N	V	KIN PL	[CAT]	N N

---

⁸All but one lexicon consulted failed to reflect the seemingly unbridled tendency for words to change grammatical function from environment to environment. The exception is Nguyễn Đinh Hoa (1991).

In a pagoda on a high mountain there was a young man who had been raised by a Buddhist monk. Daily, the Buddhist monk taught him various martial arts.

(13) Sword:41

vì	đâm	mạnh	tay	quá,	mūi	gươm
because^of	stab	be^strong	hand	excessive	point	sword
PRT	V	[SV]	N	[AJ]	[GC]	N

của	chàng	bị	gãy
possession	young^man	[NEG^PASS]	be^broken
GC	KCL	ASP	[SV]

Because of the extremely strong-handed stabbing, the point of the young man's sword was broken off.

With regard to cognitive processing, REFERENTIAL ACCESSIBILITY refers to how hearers come to identify new referents. To take in information, hearers have two options. They can associate the information about the referent with old information about the referent stored in memory, in which case they 'open' an existing cognitive file, or they can identify the information as unassociable and open a new cognitive file. Referents can be accessed on the basis of cultural understanding, awareness of the deictic context, or information given in the preceding discourse; see 3.2. In terms of syntactic marking, new information is usually coded by the speaker as indefinite; old or given information is usually coded as definite.

2
Literature Review

2.1. General overview. Classifier languages exist in all the major language areas of the world except for Europe.[9] Moreover, classifier systems appear in typologically diverse languages: analytic (Chinese), agglutinative (Swahili, Japanese), and polysynthetic (Dyirbal). Classifier systems themselves vary: there are numeral, nominal, verbal, and genitive classification systems. The inventory of classifiers in a language varies from language to language, numbering from a dozen to hundreds. The inventory of nouns which normally occur classified or unclassified also varies.[10]

Numeral classification is the most common and recognized type of classifier system and the one which is of the greatest interest for the immediate study. Numeral classification systems are used to express counting by units, measure, or sort. While a numeral classifier language may have a plural morpheme, the marking for nominal plural is generally not compulsory and is in complementary distribution with the use of classifiers.

To be identified as a numeral classifier language, a language must exhibit certain syntactic and semantic properties. The hallmark numeral classifier construction contains the constituents number + classifier +

---

[9]Strictly speaking, European languages with obligatory gender distinctions on nouns are not classifier languages. This is because gender classification is generally considered a subset of noun properties rather than a domain of semantic classification.

[10]Much of the background information in this chapter is derived from the following sources: Allan 1977:285, 291; Craig 1986; Craig 1994:565–67; Greenberg 1977:277–93; Tsou 1976:1215–16; Li and Thompson 1981; and Goral 1978.

classified noun, the order of which varies from language to language. The one alleged universal syntactic constraint on the numeral classifier construction is that no matter what order the constituents occur in, the number (or quantifier) and the classifier must always be adjacent to each other. The number or equivalent constituent in numeral classifier constructions quantifies the head noun, and the classifier classifies some aspect of the head noun. In individual languages these constraints are met to varying degrees and in various ways. For example, in Mandarin and in Kiriwina (Oceanic), a demonstrative adjective construction as well as a numeral construction requires a classifier. In Jacaltec (Mayan), a classifier can occur as a pronoun, that is, it may substitute for the entire number + classifier + noun phrase.

Since classifiers extend over some semantically heterogeneous classes, there is considerable discussion in the literature on the language-specific semantic domains of classifiers. Numeral classifier systems typically classify on the basis of shape and dimension, while nominal classifier systems categorize primarily on the basis of material and social interaction. Nominal and numeral classification systems are often referred to as one and the same system, although a language may employ more than one type of classification. Sonsorol (Oceanic) has both genitive and numeral type systems. Jacaltec exhibits nominal and numeral classification, but the two types are distinguishable on the basis of syntax. In Jacaltec, a noun classifier appears as a free morpheme adjacent to the noun and is used independently of quantification, while a numeral classifier appears bound to the number or quantifier. In a move to clarify the analysis of classifier languages, Greenberg (1977:279–80) has suggested that the two types of classifiers—nominal and numeral—represent two separate classifier systems and should be further researched as such. He also proposes that multiple classification systems in one language may be a sign of diachronic processes whereby one type of classifier develops into another type over time and use.

Works on the semantics of classifiers are numerous (including Adams, Becker, and Denny, all in Craig (ed.) 1986; Riddle 1989). Several studies concentrate on the semantic functions of classifiers in general, but most of the studies examine the semantic functions and domains for classifiers in specific languages.

Recent syntactic studies on classifier systems are less numerous than semantic studies. Lehman (1991) doubts that the main purpose for classifiers is to classify, and he provides a viable argument for viewing the classifier principally as a nominal agreement marker. Although based on evidence from Tibeto-Burman languages, the theory could also extend to classifier languages of the Austroasiatic family (particularly given the geographic proximity and typological similarities of the two families).

According to a typological assessment of eight southeast Asian classifier languages, even though some languages have areal typological features in common, the classifier systems of those languages are not necessarily similar (Goral 1978). However, some languages share similar semantic categories. In southeast Asian classifier languages, common semantic categories associated with the use of classifiers include kin, time units, and an array of other sets, including places (types of buildings) and objects (string, fruit) (Adams 1991:65).

Adams provides the most recent survey of the classifier systems in Austroasiatic languages. Among the Mon-Khmer, Nicobarese, and Aslian subfamilies, there is some historical influence from the classifier systems of Tai, Chinese, and Mon-Khmer: lexical items and semantic classes from the Tai, Chinese, and Mon-Khmer families have been borrowed or adapted to give the individual classifier systems in Austroasiatic languages their present characteristics. Tai is also the suspected primary influence on the Chinese classifier system (Erbaugh 1986; Peyraube 1991).

2.2. Numeral classifiers in Vietnamese. Vietnamese is an example of a numeral classifier language with a large group of nouns which do not necessarily need to be classified. This situation is not unusual, since numerical classifier languages almost always include in their inventories nouns which do not take a classifier (Dixon 1986:106). As with classifier systems throughout the world's languages, the Vietnamese classifier system has been analyzed principally within syntactic and semantic frameworks. The classifiers themselves are sometimes considered a subclass of noun, sometimes a member of a separate grammatical category, and are sometimes left unspecified as to syntactic category.[11]

The syntactic constraints on numeral classifier noun phrases in Vietnamese prescribe a particular word order, which is displayed in (14) (adapted from Emeneau 1951:85). The constituents other than the numerators are the basic substantive phrase. A numerated NP includes either a numerator (including quantifiers, pluralizers, and numbers) or demonstrative numerator (including demonstrative pronouns and some question words), or both. The symbol [±] indicates that an attributive constituent(s) is optional.

---

[11]See Emeneau 1951:84; Nguyễn Đinh Hoa 1957; Thompson 1965; Adams and Conklin 1973; Adams, Becker, and Conklin 1975; Dyvik 1983; Cao Xuan Hao 1988; Panfilov 1988; Honey 1956; and Stroganov 1974.

(14) Schema for numerated constructions in Vietnamese

	Classifier	Classified Noun		
Numerator			± Attribute(s)	Demonstrative
		Nonclassified Noun		Numerator

However, as early as 1951, exceptions to the classic numeral classifier construction were noted: "A numerated substantive phrase may lack a noun of the classified type yet retain the classifier, when the preceding context, verbal or other, has identified the head" (Emeneau 1951:84). Even a contemporary pedagogical grammar of colloquial Vietnamese teaches that one of the uses of a classifier is "to substitute for a noun" (Tuan and Moore 1994:66–67). The anaphoric use of classifiers is explained simply: "When you answer a question about something you can use the classifier on its own in the answer (as long as it is clear what you are talking about)" (Tuan and Moore 1994:80). Other linguists concur;[12] however, Dyvik (1983:27–28) stresses that the anaphoric use of classifiers in Vietnamese does not equal pronominal usage such as that associated with English personal pronouns.

Nguyễn Đinh Hoa (1957) presents an analysis of stress patterns in numeral classifier constructions in Vietnamese and pays special attention to categories referred to as subclasses of non-classified nouns and sub-members of special classifiers, describing the criteria for classifier use in terms of syntactic patterns and various specific denotations. Several enlightening concepts emerge from Hoa's analysis: (1) Some ordinary nouns are used as classifiers on a temporary basis and some nouns are considered quasi classifiers by virtue of their meaning; (2) some kin terms also function as classifiers; (3) classifiers are used with nouns that are described by restrictive relative clauses. I address these concerns in chapter 4.

Semantic analyses of Vietnamese classifiers have focused on the types of words with which classifiers occur and the consequent change of meaning a classifier brings to that word. At least one semantic domain—kinship-based classifiers—distinguishes Vietnamese as different from the majority of southeast Asia area classifier languages. While numeral classifier languages in the Mon-Khmer family typically exhibit classification of humans, a minority of languages have what Adams terms elaborated human classifiers. For example, instead of using a single classifier to distinguish humans from nonhumans, a speaker uses different classifiers to refer to members of different social classes:

---

[12]See Nguyễn Đinh Hoa 1957:130; Adams, Becker, and Conklin 1975; Goral 1978; Panfilov 1988.

deities, clergymen, (ordinary) men, (ordinary) persons, and so forth. Vietnamese is among the few languages which, in addition to categorizing on the basis of social and religious classes, base their human classification on kin relationships (Adams 1992:107, 113, 119–20).

In addition to imbuing the constituent it classifies with specific denotations and shades of meaning, classifiers perform a wide range of grammatical functions. Classifiers in Vietnamese are said to individuate and disambiguate concepts, introduce relative clauses, nominalize forms, add definiteness, mark possession, and substitute for nouns.

Cao Xuan Hao (1988) voices notable dissent against most other analyses. According to Cao, the basis of the classifier system in Vietnamese is the semantic distinction between count nouns and mass nouns.[13] Further, classifiers as a grammatical category should not be considered as adjuncts to nouns proper; rather, they specify the count/mass distinction from the point of view of native speakers of Vietnamese. He notes that the reason why the Vietnamese classifier system remains a mystery is that Indo-European linguists too frequently analyze not the Vietnamese phrase or word itself, but its French, English, or Russian translation (Cao 1988:38, 41, 46–47).

Dyvik (1983:9) writes on the "primacy of the syntactical function of classifiers, whose semantic import is...that of individuation." He stresses the need for "a set of terms to refer to specific syntactic functions (such as individuator) as distinct from the set of terms denoting syntactical and lexical categories (such as classifier and noun)" (1983:17). While Dyvik's study is focused on syntactic functions rather than discourse functions of classifiers, it is nonetheless a stepping stone from discussions of the semantic nature or syntactic environment of classifiers to their functional aspects. His study is based on interviews the analyst conducted with two native speakers, in which he elicited their intuitions regarding the grammaticality of classifier phrases presented within a set of written syntactic frames. The result was a list of syntactic structures associated with classifiers, and a set of phrase structure and assignment rules which generate the structures. Such a study is valuable in that it provides a list of the possible syntactic constructions containing classifiers; however, it still leaves unanswered the question of why classifiers are used. By focusing only on the sentence-level syntactic properties of classifiers, Dyvik leaves open the possibility of analyzing classifiers in the larger context of natural language—discourse.

2.3. Classifiers in discourse. Only a handful of studies have been done on the discourse use of classifiers in classifier languages; Downing,

---

[13]T'sou 1976:1220 also mentions the count-mass distinction as one feature of the classifier systems in Asian languages.

Becker, and Hopper (all in Craig (ed.), 1986) and Riddle (1989) represent recent works I found in English on the discourse use of classifiers in various languages. The present study is perhaps the first discourse-based study of classifiers in Vietnamese.

Among classifier languages, "alternation of the classifier morphemes with nouns and their objects is not unusual" (Adams 1986:242). Classifiers are used anaphorically in a number of languages, including Thai, Vietnamese, Japanese, Burmese, and Jacaltec. One notable function attributed to classifiers in non-numeral constructions in Thai is foregrounding the noun. Classifiers are used in reference to particular individuals and are deleted when reference to those individuals is not wanted. New topics are introduced by classifier constructions in Japanese and Burmese.

Downing (1986:349, 356) reports on the behavior of classifiers in Japanese written narrative and conversation, concentrating her analysis on the anaphoric behavior of the various forms. Several findings make this study significant. First, she found that there is a marked difference between the frequency of human and nonhuman classifiers, the human classifiers occurring overwhelmingly more often than the other type. Second, nonhuman classifiers are not used anaphorically at all in the Japanese data, although informants cited them with demonstratives (without nouns) in elicited examples. Third, anaphoric classifiers in Japanese can be used a longer distance from the antecedent than the anaphor-antecedent distance allowable for pronouns and ellipses. Finally, human classifiers are used when the speaker wants to express a post-initial mention of a referent in a neutral way. All of these observations are impossible to discern from lower level syntactic or lexico-semantic studies.

Riddle (1989) reports that in White Hmong, noun classifiers perform the semantic function of individuation commonly attributed to classifiers. According to her findings, in discourse in White Hmong, the individuation function is manifest as referential salience. In this function, classifiers are used to increase the precision of reference, thereby emphasizing the relative salience of their referents from the speaker's point of view.

These studies indicate that whether introducing a new referent, foregrounding a referent, or marking a subject's or object's referential salience, the use of classifier constructions cannot be understood outside of the discourse environment.

2.4. Previous discourse studies on Vietnamese. In the literature on Vietnamese I found just one investigation done from a discourse perspective. Clark (1992) conducted a study of the conjunction *thì* 'then' as a topicalizer in Vietnamese. In it, the concept topic pertains to information which is presupposed or given, and a topicalizer refers to the constituent which marks the topic. Topic as considered in Clark's study differs from the understanding of topic for the present research. Consequently, the two studies are relevant to each other only inasmuch as both employ an overall discourse-based approach to the same language.

2.5. Summary. Previous studies of classifiers in Vietnamese by others already cited have concentrated primarily on the syntactic and lexico-semantic structure of classifier systems and have analyzed the system on the basis of syntactic and semantic categories and functions. From these studies it is apparent that Vietnamese is clearly a classifier language with a large inventory of classifiers, although the actual inventory of words which should be counted as classifiers is debatable; see appendix A. There is also debate over which words, if any, should be considered nonclassified nouns, though some nouns appear unclassified at least some of the time. Classifiers appear in constructions with and without numbers, with and without nouns, and with and without demonstratives. In addition, they can function as pronouns, although no details concerning this anaphoric role have been stated in the literature.

The use of kin classifiers in referent tracking has also been overlooked. Kin classifiers are specifically used to refer to humans, which often tend to be topical in discourse. The topicality of kin classifiers compared to nonkin classifiers, and the significance of their topicality, can only be grasped in contexts larger than the sentence. Likewise, the appropriateness of definite or indefinite reference can only be grasped in the larger context. Classifier constructions in Vietnamese sometimes represent definite referents and sometimes indefinite referents, but no statement has been made as to the reason for their distribution in discourse. As mentioned above, classifier constructions in Japanese are used to introduce new referents into discourse; this may also be the case in Vietnamese.

In addition to the functions already mentioned, classifiers are sometimes used to nominalize forms, and they are optionally used with relative clauses and as markers of possession. The logic of these seemingly scattered and unrelated uses can be understood when they are viewed as part of a system operating in natural context.

3
Methodology

In this investigation I tested four hypotheses with regard to classifier functions in Vietnamese narrative texts. To address the hypothesis that classifiers do not obligatorily occur with numbers, I took an inventory of numbers and classifiers in the data and compared their distribution. Based on simple tallies, I determined the frequency with which the words in each of these two word classes appear in the same or in a separate syntactic construction. To test the second hypothesis that most classifier constructions in Vietnamese do not conform to the prototypical syntactic pattern of number + classifier + noun, I again employed simple tallies, this time of all the types of NPs in the data. The assumption behind comparing distribution frequencies is that the prototypical numeral classifier construction is the most frequently encountered of all syntactic patterns associated with classifiers. Consequently, if one can show that the prototype in question does not occur more frequently than the other patterns, then one has established a reason to doubt its status as the prototype.

With regard to the third hypothesis that Vietnamese exhibits greater similarity to White Hmong than to Japanese in terms of shared classifier discourse functions, I compared the use of classifiers in the discourse of these two languages to the use of classifiers in Vietnamese, based on the fact that cross-linguistically, language systems (in this instance, classification) share similarities.

In addressing the fourth hypothesis (that referential salience is the single discourse function that accounts for all the other classifier functions), I examined the data for evidence of specific classifier functions. I tested both the third and fourth hypotheses by assessing NPs in the data with regard to referential accessibility (RA), and using the textual measurements of referent continuity (RC), referential distance (RD), and referential persistence (RP). With these measurements, which are adapted from Givón (1983, 1984a, 1990), I was able to determine instances in which the classifiers in the data function as markers of definiteness, as markers of referent continuity or discontinuity, and as markers of thematically important referents. For example, to determine the validity of the claim that classifiers function as markers of definiteness, I used RA to determine the definiteness of all the NPs, then counted the distribution of definite NPs in relation to the distribution of classified NPs. Last, I deduced patterns from the textual statistics to form my conclusions.

3.1. The corpus. The data used for this study are four Vietnamese folk tales published with English free translations.[14] The folklore is estimated to have originated prior to the fifteenth century, although exact dates for these four stories were not available at the time of this study. The contemporary writers of these stories are likely to have come from the southern part of Vietnam, given demographic and social factors affecting the Vietnamese population in the past twenty years. However, the genre itself originates in the north (Barker p.c.; Gregerson and Gregerson p.c.). While there are marked phonological differences between contemporary spoken northern and southern Vietnamese dialects, their written discourse contains few differences in lexical items and idioms, and no obvious differences with regard to discourse features. However, within the genre of narrative folk tales, at least a few discourse features and specialized expressions are employed. For example, a folk tale or a legend typically begins with the equivalent of 'once upon a time', ng y xưa. Terms such as n ng 'damsel' and quan 'mandarin' (a rank of public official during the time of feudal Vietnam) are particular to folk tales, although the latter term is also used in historical accounts. Many of the characters and themes also identify the works as folk tales. Three of the four stories used in this research depict queens, kings, and princesses (legendary or historical) as major or minor characters; two of the stories involve characters with magical powers; and the conflict in one of the stories centers around the slaying of a python, an animal depicted similarly to the dragons of European medieval folklore. Two of the stories give mythical explanations of phenomena in the natural world, for example, one story explains the origin of mosquitoes.

---

[14]The two volumes from which the narratives are taken were published by National Textbook Company and contain a total of thirteen stories (Trần Van Điền and Lê Tinh Thông 1992; Trần Van Điền and Trần Cảnh Xuân 1993).

Methodology

The texts consist of 636 to 842 words each, and appear in volumes that were intended as reading books for adolescent-aged children (approximately twelve years and older) of Vietnamese speaking families in the United States. The books were written by Vietnamese educators for use in bilingual or multicultural programs.

The corpus consists of four texts: *A Broken Sword, Son Tinh and Thuy Tinh* (Trần Van Điền and Trần Cảnh Xuân 1993), *Mission Impossible*, and *The Story of the Mosquito* (Trần Van Điền and L Tinh Thông 1992), all of which appear in Vietnamese with English glosses, free translations, and grammatical tags as well as a plot summary for each in appendix B. Throughout this study, I refer to each story using an abbreviated form of its title, as listed in (15).

(15) Title of text   Abbreviated title

     A Broken Sword   Sword
     Mission Impossible   Mission
     Son Tinh and Thuy Tinh   Tinh
     The Story of the Mosquito   Mosquito

I chose these particular texts because they contain a variety of nouns for which I know specific classifiers exist in Vietnamese. For example, *Tinh* mentions fruit, trees, and animals, for which possible classifiers are *quả* 'fruit', *cây* 'tree', and *con* 'nonhuman living being' or *lo i* 'species'. Another reason I chose these texts was because each of them has at least three classifiers that are used five or more times each. The use of classifiers in relation to referential continuity is the focus of two of my hypotheses, so it is important to have several classifiers that are used repeatedly in an individual story. This increases the likelihood of finding classifiers functioning anaphorically as pronouns. If the same classifier is used a number of times in the same text, the classifier in question may refer to the same referent, thus playing a part in the referential continuity of the story. In addition to the classifier inventory, I chose these texts because they each contain several cardinal numbers. Since one of my hypotheses tests whether or not the use of a cardinal number requires a classifier, it is necessary to have cardinal number constructions in the data.

Two of the texts contain approximately 650 words, and two texts contain approximately 850 words. The length of a text has little bearing on the number of classifiers it contains because the number of classifiers depends not on word counts, but on referential continuity in relation to thematically important referents. (Referential continuity in relation to the use of classifiers is discussed in 4.7–4.10.) To illustrate this point statistically, the averages for classifiers used in each text are shown in (16)–(18). The corpus contains 714 noun phrases, and 50 different classifiers used 296 times in total. The classifiers are listed in appendix A with the number of times they occur in each text. In addition to these four texts, I also consulted other narratives for examples to confirm or refute the hypotheses because some classifiers occur infrequently in these four texts.

Of the fifty classifiers used, thirteen are modifying classifiers (MC) and thirty-seven are general categoricals (GC) as charted in (16). Although the discourse functions of classifiers contradict a syntactic description which assumes the subtypes MC and GC, the grammatical unit field is left marked for both MC and GC in all the texts to demonstrate the contrast between their syntactic description and their textual distribution and usage. All four texts in appendix B are tagged with the MC-GC distinction.

(16) Number of different classifiers in the four texts

Text	# MC types	# GC types	# MC & GC types	# classifier tokens	# of words in texts
Sword	6	23	29	93	842
Mission	2	13	15	78	636
Tinh	4	18	22	60	838
Mosquito	5	14	19	65	655
# of each type in all texts	13	37	50	296	2971
Average # per text	4.25	17	21.25	74	743

The fact that the overall number of classifier tokens which occur in the text (broken down by text in column four of (16)) exceeds the number of NPs which contain a classifier, shown in column two of (17), indicates that some NPs contain more than one classifier. Since I am concerned with the frequency with which classifiers occur in certain types of NPs, the figures in in column two of (17) are of greater interest to this study than the figures in column four of (16).

Methodology

(17) NPs with and without classifiers

Text	#NPs	#NPs containing a classifier	%NPs containing a classifier
Sword	203	83	41%
Mission	155	66	43%
Tinh	208	50	24%
Mosquito	148	40	27%
Total	714	239	average: 34%

The figures in (18) list the number of occurrences (tokens) of MCs and GCs in the texts as distinct from the number of different MC or GC types in (16) and the number of classifier NPs in (17).

(18) Number of MC and GC tokens in each text

#of tokens	Sword	Mission	Tinh	Mosquito	Total for all texts	Average per text
#MC tokens each text	20	14	8	10	52	13
#GC tokens each text	73	64	52	55	244	61
Total classifier tokens	93	78	60	65	296	74

3.2–3.5 Methodology

The investigation was carried out in four phases: (1) data preparation and coding, (2) quantitative distribution analysis, (3) discourse analysis of reference, and (4) cross-linguistic comparison. In the first phase, I prepared and coded the data by glossing the texts, assigning grammatical tags, determining clause breaks, identifying the constituents that are relevant to the study, and coding for definiteness and given versus new information. For the second phase, I counted the number of NPs and grouped them according to their syntactic construction type, then counted the NPs that contain the number one, distinguishing definite from indefinite NPs. In phase two, I also compared the syntactic properties of MCs to those of GCs, and examined the anaphoric use of classifiers. In phase three, I measured several textual features in relation to classifiers. These features are referential continuity, overall frequency, referential distance, and referential persistence. For the final phase of the study, I compared the findings of the study by Downing (1986) on the anaphoric functions of classifiers in Japanese to my findings on the anaphoric functions for Vietnamese, and applied four criteria that are used to identify classifier functions in White Hmong to several portions of the Vietnamese texts. Each of these phases is described in greater detail in the following sections.

3.2. Data preparation and coding. The data preparation and coding phase consisted of six steps. Steps one and two consisted of glossing and assigning grammatical tags, and could be done simultaneously. I used Vietnamese and English dictionaries when filling in single-morpheme and compound glosses of each word in the texts. I also consulted with several speakers of Vietnamese to check the accuracy of the glossing and grammatical tagging. I used the parameters for the grammatical categories described in the Vietnamese reference grammar by Thompson (1965) in assigning a grammatical tag to each morpheme. This reference grammar is the most comprehensive descriptive linguistic account of modern Vietnamese written in English. The constituents of greatest interest in the present analysis are: modifying classifiers (MC), general categoricals (GC), nouns (N), kin terms (KIN), and numbers (NU). Where the grammatical category of a word is ambiguous or changes with its immediate context, I placed brackets around the grammatical tag. For example, in (19), *lúc* 'moment' fits the syntactic description for a MC in Thompson (1965), but is not explicitly listed there. Therefore, its grammatical tag is bracketed: [MC]. Likewise, *vi n* 'official' fits the description for the grammatical category (GC) in the reference grammar, but is not among the few examples listed there (Thompson 1965). The verb *còn* 'remain' functions primarily as the conventional grammatical category of adverb, a category which is absent from the reference grammar. The words *t i* 'beˆpale' and *x m* 'beˆgrey' function sometimes as adjectives (also not in the reference grammar) and sometimes as verbs, so they receive the bracketed label [SV] for stative verb.

(19) Sword:59

Lúc	*đó,*	*mặt*	*vi n*	*l nh*	*tuần*	*t i*	*x m,*
moment	that	face	official	patrolman	patrol	beˆpale	beˆgrey
[MC]	DM	N	[GC]	N	V	[SV]	[SV]

cắt	không	còn	một	giọt	m u
cut^off	not	remain	one/a	droplet	blood
V	NG	[V]	NU	MC	N

That moment, the patrolman's face turned pale, as if cut off so that not one droplet of blood remained in it.

The third step in preparing the data for analysis involved using the reference grammar to identify the clauses and NPs. NPs and clauses form the basic units used for the textual measurements, so identifying them is prerequisite to the analysis. In addition to Thompson (1965), I applied principles from Givón (1983, 1984a, 1990) with regard to distinctions between types of clauses. For the textual measurements, it is necessary to distinguish two types of clauses, main and relative. In Vietnamese, main clauses may be independent, as in (20); they may be joined to another clause by a coordinating conjunction, as in (21), or they may be joined to another clause without a conjunction, as in (22). In instances where two clauses are joined without a conjunction, the relationship between the clauses must be assessed in terms of interclausal coherence in order to determine whether or not one clause is subordinate to the other.

(20) Sword:34

Ch ng	lanh	tay	chém	một	ph t	v o	đầu
young^man	be^agile	hand	chop	one/a	whack	enter	head
[KCL]	[SV]	N	V	NU	N	[V]	N

The deft young man struck one blow to the (python's) head.

(21) Sword:15, 16

Đó	l	đền	của	mãng	x	m	cậu	không	hay.
that	be	temple	possession	boa	snake	but	3s	not	know
DM	CP	N	GC	N	N	PRT	KIN	NG	V

That was the python's temple **but** he did not know it.

(22) Sword:13, 14

Tr n đường	về	l ng		qu ,	ch ng
on road	return	native^village	countryside		young^man
RN N	[V]	GC	N		KCL

thanh ni n	gặp	một	ngôi	đền,	bèn
youth <	< encounter	one	temple	temple	immediately
N> <	V	NU	[MC]	N	AV

ghé	v o	nghỉ	chân.
stop^off^at	enter	rest	foot/leg
V	[V]	V	N

On the way back to his native village, the young man came upon a temple and immediately stopped in to rest his legs.

(23) Sword:5

Con	qu i	vật	mỗi	ng y	một	trở	n n
animal	monster	creature	every	day	one	become	<
MC	[SV]	N	PL	GC	NU	CP	<

hung		dữ,	gây	kinh		ho ng	cho
be^fierce^looking		< bring		be^frightened		fear	for/until
[SV]		<	V	[SV]		N	CJ

cả	vùng.
all/the^whole	region
PRT	N

Every day the monster became more fearsome, bringing terror to the whole region.

To distinguish two main clauses from a main and a subordinate clause, I used principles associated with interclausal coherence from Givón (1990). For example, in (22) and (23), the clauses are joined without a conjunction. These examples illustrate similar syntax, with an explicit subject in the first clause, a comma separating the two clauses, and an elliptical subject in the second clause. Although neither sentence exhibits much syntactic marking, the level of clause integration can be determined by the semantic connections between them. In terms of temporal continuity, the action of the clauses in (22) are sequential, making the clauses more distinct, while the action of the clauses in (23) are concurrent, making them more closely linked. Consequently, I considered example (22) to illustrate two main clauses, and example (23) to illustrate a main clause joined with a subordinate clause. Although I do not discuss the larger discourse environment with the present examples, each clause should be considered not only in relation to its immediately adjacent clauses, but also in relation to discourse as a whole, because interclausal coherence is a subset of overall discourse coherence.

Aside from main clauses, one must distinguish relative clauses. In syntactic terms, in Vietnamese, a relative clause is a subordinate clause that modifies a main clause noun, as in (24).

(24) Sword:8

Nh	vua	cũng	hứa	ai	**giết**	**chế**	**con**	**măng**
respected	king	likewise	promise	anyone	kill	die	animal	boa
GC	N	PRT	V	IDN	V	V	MC	N

x	sẽ	được		cưới	công	chúa.	
snake	shall	finish^successfully		marry	princess	<	
N	[MD]	ASP		V	N	<	

The king also promised that whoever **killed the python** would marry the princess.

Vietnamese employs little syntactic marking of case roles other than word order, so in instances such as (25), where the semantic case role of the head noun in the main clause differs from that of the restrictive relative clause, syntactic marking of the verb is employed. In (25), an aspect marker is used as an additional indicator to the semantic case role of the noun in the relative clause (patient) which differs from the semantic case role of the main clause noun (agent) with which it co-refers.

(25) Sword:9

Thời	bấy	giờ,	có	ch ng	thanh	ni n	**được**
then/time	then	time	exist	young^man	youth	<	[PASSIVE]
N	DM	GC	V	KCL	N>	<	ASP

	một	*nh*		*sư*		*nuôi*	*dưỡng*	*ở*
	one	respected		Buddhist^monk		rear	support	be^located^in/at
	NU	[GC]		N		V	V	[SV]

	một	*ngôi*	*chùa*	*tr n*	*núi*		*cao.*
	one	temple	temple	on	mountain		be^high
	NU	[MC]	N	RN	N		[SV]

At that time, there was a young man **who had been raised by a Buddhist monk in a pagoda on a high mountain.**

The fourth step in the data preparation and coding phase was identifying NPs and isolating the number NPs. In terms of word order typology, Vietnamese is a rigid SVO (subject-verb-object) language. Thus, in simple clauses, as illustrated in example (20) and reproduced in (26), the expectation is that there would be noun phrases in the subject and object positions. In (26) there are three NPs. The subject NP is *ch ng lanh tay* 'deft young man', the main clausal object is *một ph t* 'one blow', and the secondary object is *đầu* 'head'.

(26) Sword:34

	Ch ng	*lanh*	*tay*	*chém*	*một*	*ph t*	*v o*	*đầu*
	young^man	be^agile	hand	chop	one/a	whack	enter	head
	[KCL]	[SV]	N	V	NU	N	[V]	N
	S			V		O		
	The deft young man			struck	one blow		to the (python's) head.	

Steps five and six of the data preparation phase involved coding NPs for two discourse relations, referential accessibility (definiteness) and information status (given versus new). The significance of referentiality to this study lies in its relationship to focus and topic importance. An entity must be referential before it can be focused on or considered thematically important, and an entity's definiteness or indefiniteness is an indicator of its local or discourse-wide level of thematic importance. The definiteness of a referent is partly determined by its status as given or new information.

I evaluated the referential accessibility of NPs in terms of cognitive processing of given versus new information. (In this discussion, speaker and hearer in relation to written discourse refers to writer and reader, respectively.) A hearer may access an already existing cognitive file for

Methodology

a referent based on prior cultural knowledge, prior mention of the entity in the discourse, or connections from the deictic context. If the hearer can access the information as an already existing cognitive file, it is given information, and the NP is generally coded as definite. Conversely, when a hearer cannot identify a referent, it is inaccessible, or new information. As a result, the hearer must open a new cognitive file for the new information, and the NP is typically coded as indefinite in order to signal this need. The RA categories based on referentiality factors are listed in (27).

(27) Categories of referential accessibility

Referential Accessibility	Inaccessible information	Accessible information		
Coding for Definiteness	Indefinite	Definite		
Category	I	II	III	IV
Referentiality Factors	the NP is inaccessible, newly introduced	the NP is accessible through prior cultural knowledge or its generic nature	the NP is evident from the deictic context	the NP was mentioned previously in the discourse and cognitively speaking, the NP is within a retrievable range

In terms of communication, when the speaker is talking about a specific, referential entity, and the speaker believes that the hearer can identify that same entity, the speaker syntactically codes the NP as definite (RA category numbers II, III, or IV in (27)). If the speaker is talking about a specific, referential entity, and the speaker believes that the hearer cannot identify that same specific entity, the speaker syntactically codes the NP as indefinite (RA category I). When the NP is coded as indefinite, the hearer must open a new cognitive file for that entity. While it is not possible to know what is in the mind of the speaker or hearer, it is possible to determine the definiteness of NPs by applying the cognitive principles just explained. The RA factor for which I, as a third party to the discourse (and as a cultural outsider), suffer the greatest lack of knowledge is that portion of category II which is associated with prior cultural knowledge. However, I can analyze the referential accessibility and information status of the NPs in a text based on previous occurrences of the same referent in the discourse, their syntactic marking, my understanding of the deictic situation and generic knowledge of the world.

According to Givón (1990:922), definite NPs tend to receive more grammatical marking, thus indicating a higher level of thematic importance. Unfortunately, Vietnamese does not have grammatical devices which consistently mark the definite-indefinite distinction of an individual NP. However, the semantic definiteness of an NP can be evaluated by its status as given or new information. If the referent appears in the preceding discourse environment in any form (e.g., full NP, proper noun, pronoun), the NP in question is given, and likely to be definite in the estimation of the speaker. If the NP is the first occurrence of the referent in the discourse, the NP is new information, and is likely to be indefinite in the estimation of the speaker. In addition to this, if the number one appears with the newly introduced referent and is not being used as a cardinal number, it is likely that the number signifies the indefiniteness of the NP.

Shared knowledge about the universe can also be used to determine an NP's definiteness. Consider the NP *một mạng người con g i* 'one life of young girl' in (28). In the preceding discourse, a python had been terrorizing a kingdom by eating the people and livestock in it. In order to protect his kingdom, the king builds the python a temple, and, as presented in (28), promises to make a human sacrifice to it once a year.

(28) Sword:7

v	hứa	h ng	năm	dâng		nó	một	mạng
and	promise	row	year	offer^respectfully		3s^ARROG	one	life
CJ	V	[N]	GC	V		PRO	NU	N

người	con	g i	để		nó	thuần	t nh
person	offspring	girl	in^order^to		3s^ARROG	be^tamed	disposition
GC	GC	N	CJ		PRO	[SV]	N

lại.
again
[AV]

...and promised to offer it **the life of a young girl** every year in order for it to be tame again.

The appearance of the bolded NP in (28) is the first in the discourse, so the referent is likely to be inaccessible and hence can be considered indefinite. The NP also contains the number one; however, since the NP is comprised of two nominals, *mạng* 'life' and *người con gi* 'young girl', one must decide to which nominal the number refers. If I assume the number refers to the head of the NP *mạng* 'life', the meaning of the phrase would be 'one life of (a) young girl'. However, we all know that every person has one life, and, barring that this story is about reincarnation, 'one life per person' is accessible, given information. Therefore, we should consider *mạng* 'life' definite. Although the literal translation of *con g i* is 'daughter', the classifier *người* 'person' categorizes the referent as 'one unit of the class *con g* ' and thus leaves the number one to code the NP as indefinite.

In terms of dialogue, I determined a referent's RA by its relationship to the speaker and hearer in the dialogue, rather than by the referent's relationship to the narrator and reader of the text. For example, an NP might have already been introduced in the narrative, so is old information to the reader; yet that same NP may be a new mention to the character being addressed in dialogue in the text. In this case, I consider the referent inaccessible information and, therefore, indefinite.

In step six of the data preparation phase, along with determining the given or new status of each NP in the data, I identified each initial mention of a referent based on its position in the text. For example, if a referent is mentioned in clauses 2 and 3, and clauses 10 and 13, the NP in clause 2 is an initial mention.

3.3. Quantitative distribution analysis. The quantitative distribution phase of the procedures consisted of five steps. Each step involved counting the frequency of specific syntactic constructions or constituents. For step one, I counted all the NPs in the four texts. Next, I counted every NP that contains a classifier, then every NP that contains a number. An NP is considered classified if it contains a classifier, regardless of the other constituents in the construction. For example, classifier + noun, number + classifier, or classifier are all classifier constructions. The same principle applies to number NPs. NPs that contain a classifier and a number are counted in both categories for this part of the analysis. I also counted the commonly prescribed numeral classifier construction: number + classifier + noun. Example (29) shows the prototypical construction.

(29) Sword:59

    Lúc   đó, mặt vi n   l nh   tuần t i   x m,
    moment that face official patrolman patrol be^pale be^grey
    [MC]   DM N   [GC]   N   V   [SV]   [SV]

    cắt   không còn   một   giọt   m u
    cut^off not   remain one/a droplet blood
    V   NG   [V]   NU   MC   N

That moment, the patrolman's face turned pale, as if cut off so that not **one droplet of blood** remained in it.

    In terms of overall frequency within each text, I compared the tallies of classifier constructions, numeral constructions, and the prototypical numeral classifier constructions with each other and calculated the percentage of each category contained in each text. With these figures I include a tally of NPs which contain both a number and a classifier. These figures help me answer the first and second hypotheses; they show whether or not the use of a number requires a classifier, and they show whether or not the prototypical numeral classifier construction is the most frequently used in discourse.

    Step two of the quantitative analysis phase is also designed to address the first and second hypotheses. To carry out step two, I placed the tallies of every numeral construction type (e.g., number + noun, or number + classifier, etc.) in a table, grouping the counts by the number in the NP and by the text in which each construction appears. By grouping the tallies by number, I am able to see any marked statistical differences between the use of each number; and by grouping the tallies by text, I am able to see any marked statistical differences between the texts with regard to the numbers used.

    Step three of the quantitative distribution phase consists of subdividing the tallies from step two: the totals for each number are grouped by their uses in discourse. The purpose of this procedure is to search for a correlation between the presence of classifiers in numeral NPs and the functions of the numbers in those same NPs. To determine the use of a number, one must examine the individual number in relation to the discourse. For example, the number 'one' may be used as a cardinal number, as in (30). Based on the preceding discourse, I know that the speaker (*ch u* 'young relative') is not referring to just any one buffalo and any one bag of rice; the number 'one' is not being used as a marker of indefiniteness in (30). In the preceding discourse, the town elders are given three male buffaloes and two bags of rice with which to produce nine more buffaloes, or face harsh penalties. In (30), *ch u* is addressing the elders with his idea about resolving the problem, referring specifically to any 'one' of the same three buffaloes mentioned in the preceding discourse, and any 'one' of the same two bags of rice mentioned earlier. In the succeeding discourse, *ch u* gives instructions for handling the other two buffaloes and the other bag of rice, thus dispelling any residual doubt about the use of 'one' in (30); it is clearly used as a cardinal number.

(30) Mission:17

Xin	*giao*	*cho*	*ch u*	*một*	*con*	*trâu*	*v*
request	entrust	for	[young^relative]	one	animal	buffalo	and
V	V	CJ	KIN	NU	MC	N	CJ

một bao gạo.
one bag rice
NU GC N

Please give me **one buffalo** and **one bag of rice**.

A number may also function as part of an idiomatic expression, such as the way 'one' is used in (31), or as part of a compound form, such as the way 'two' is used in (32). In addition to the discourse environment, one may use the phonological characteristics of a number (spoken in context) to determine its function. Phonologically, a number in an idiomatic expression or a compound form is more closely integrated with the other constituents in its NP than a number used as a cardinal number. This is in accordance with an iconicity principle associated with morphology: "Semantic...features that are closely associated with each other also tend to co-lexicalize" (Givón 1984a). Tight phonological integration of a number with the other constituents in an NP is also associated with the number 'one' used as an indefinite article. In (32), 'one' is used two times as an indefinite article.

(31) Mosquito:35

Lúc	đầu	n ng	**một mực**	từ	chối.
moment	beginning	damsel	**one** level	renounce	refuse
[GC]	N	KCL	NU N	V	V

At first, she **steadfastly** refused.

(32) Mosquito:1

Ng y	xưa	tại	một	ngôi	l ng	nhỏ	có	**hai**	vợ
day	past	beˆat/in	one	house	village	small	exist	**two**	wife
GC	AJ	[SV]	NU	[MC]	GC	AJ	V	NU	N

chồng	trẻ	sống	trong	một	căn	nh	chật
husband	young	beˆalive	within	one	house	dwelling	cramped
N	AJ	[SV]	[PRE]	NU	[GC]	N	AJ

h p.
narrow
AJ

Once upon a time in a small village there lived a young **couple** in a cramped house.

In addition to phonological integration of the number with its NP, the status of the NP as new, and by process of elimination, the use of 'one' as a noncardinal number and as independent of an idiomatic expression or compound form, all signal the use of 'one' as an indefinite article. Since (32) is the first clause in the story, *ngôi l ng nhỏ* 'small village' and *căn nh chật h p* 'cramped house' are first mentions, and therefore, new information. Neither the village nor the house are mentioned in the succeeding ten clauses, nor are they contrasted in number with any other villages or houses; this indicates that they are presented in (32) without emphasis on the specific number of villages and houses. The use of 'one' in both NPs marks the referents as indefinite.

After separating the totals for each number into groups based on their use in the texts, one can determine the frequency with which a number is accompanied by a classifier when the number is used as a cardinal number, in an idiomatic expression, or in a compound form, or in some other capacity by calculating the percentages related to each sum. For instance, the number 'one' is used forty-seven times

Methodology

throughout all the texts, and of those forty-seven occurrences, it is used as an indefinite marker thirty times, or 64% of the time. At this point in the analysis, one can also look for particular classifier uses with respect to number use. For example, the statistics calculated thus far may indicate that every numeral NP containing the number fifty or greater contains a classifier. If such a pattern is shown by the figures, one examines each individual instance in context and notes the use of the classifier in each one.

The purpose of step four of the quantitative distribution phase is to determine whether there is a statistical correlation between classifiers and the marking of initial mentions, and classifiers and the marking of definite NPs. It is a principle of cross-linguistic discourse analysis that initial mentions of important referents tend to be indefinite. Consequently, for this procedure initial and post-initial mentions are counted and the number of classified NPs which are definite or indefinite in each of the two categories is also counted. Once each category has been counted, the figures are interpreted in terms of the principles associated with referential coherence.

Step five of the quantitative distribution phase addresses the fourth hypothesis, which states that individual syntactic or semantic classifier functions can account for only some of the use of classifiers in Vietnamese, and, conversely, that there is a single discourse function of classifiers that can account for the diverse syntactic and semantic functions. In step five, I measured the frequency with which classifiers are used as pronouns in the data. This measurement is important for determining whether or not "substituting for a noun" is a genuine classifier function in Vietnamese, and the extent to which the function is valid. For this tally, I counted classifiers that are used anaphorically, where anaphoric reference is "reference back to a person, time, or place which has just been mentioned or somehow otherwise called to attention" (Thompson 1965). Also included in this count are classifiers that are functioning as nouns—they do not refer back to or forward to another syntactic form of the same referent. For example, the classifier l ng 'village' in (33) is the first mention of the village in the narrative, yet it functions as a noun in the NP. Note also the pronominal use of the classifier đứa 'lower status' whose antecedent appears in the preceding clause.

(33) Mission:10

Nh	vua	nói	với	vị	cố-vấn,	'Người	hãy
respected	king	tell	toward	revered	advisor	person	be^sure^to
GC	N	V	PRE	[GC]	N	GC	[MD]

đem	ba	con	trâu	đực	v	ba	bao	gạo	tới	l ng
take	three	animal	buffalo	male	and	three	bag	rice	to	village
V	NU	MC	N	AJ	CJ	NU	GC	N	[V]	GC

đứa	bé	đó.
[lower^rank]	small	there
MC	AJ	DM

The king said to the advisor, "You must take three male buffaloes and three bags of rice to **that little boy's village.**"

3.4. Discourse analysis of reference. The third phase, which consists of four steps, considers classifiers in Vietnamese discourse with regard to reference. If, as I hypothesize, the discourse function that accounts for the use of classifiers in Vietnamese is related to salience of reference, the textual measurements should show that classifiers are used with the most salient referents in terms of referent continuity and referent importance.

In step one I counted the number of NPs from each of six referential strategies used in one Vietnamese text and listed them in a table. The purpose of this step is to identify the most preferred strategies of referring, and to observe where classifier NPs rank in that hierarchy. The place of classifiers in the hierarchy gives a clue as to the type of referents to which they refer. For example, classifiers may be used as often as pronouns, but not as often as unclassified nouns. In such a case, one might expect that classifiers refer to already introduced, continuous referents, as pronouns do.

In order to be consistent with the total number of tokens counted for the RD and RP tallies, NPs in quoted material and relative clauses are also omitted for this count. Therefore, excluding the quoted material and relative clauses, instead of 203 total NPs and 83 classifier NPs, the text has 192 total NPs and 70 classifier NPs. Because of the findings in phase two, for phase three I no longer distinguish between MCs and GCs, but count all classifiers as members of one word class. The nonclassifier referential categories counted are kin terms, pronouns, zero anaphora, nouns, and miscellaneous nouns. The group of miscellaneous nouns

Methodology 41

includes the few proper nouns, honorific terms, and nominalized verbs in the data. The use of only certain nouns—as opposed to all nouns—as proper nouns skew the trends related to unclassified nouns. To avoid skewing of the statistics, the statistics associated with nouns like *vua* 'king', which are consistently used as proper nouns, are grouped with another definite-referential category—proper nouns and honorifics.

In the text used for this phase of analysis (*A Broken Sword*), the noun *vua* 'king' was considered a proper noun because of its behavior in discourse. The king is referred to early in the narrative as given information. His initial mention occurs in clause 6 (34). As one of the main characters, he can be expected to be introduced by a device such as the existential presentative construction used for the initial mention of the hero in clause 9 (35). Since the folk tale is an important and long-standing genre in Vietnamese culture, the recurrence of characters such as the king are thus understood as given information, without special introduction into the discourse.

(34) Sword:6

Vua	thấy	vậy	phải	sai	dựng	một	ngôi	đền	cho
king	perceive	so	must	command	build	one	temple	temple	for
N	V	DM	[MD]	V	V	NU	[MC]	N	CJ

nó	ở
3s^ARROG	live
PRO	V

The king, perceiving this, had to order them to build a temple for it to live in.

(35) Sword:9

Thời	bấy	giờ	có	ch ng		thanh ni n	được	một
time	then	time	exist	young^man		youth <	[PASSIVE]	one/a
N	N	GC	V	KCL		N> <	ASP	NU

nh	sư		nuôi	dưỡng	ở		một
respected	Buddhist^monk		rear	support	be^located^at		one/a
GC	N		V	V	[SV]		NU

ngôi	*chùa*	*tr n*	*núi*	*cao*	
temple	temple	on/upon	mountain	beˆhigh	
MC	N	RN	N	[SV]	

At that time, **there was a young man** who had been raised by a monk in a pagoda on a high mountain.

An additional feature which characterizes reference to the king in *A Broken Sword* is that he is never referred to by a pronoun. This, like the treatment of the king as given information, is likely to be due to sociocultural factors. Their deep respect for the king may forbid Vietnamese speakers from reducing reference to the king to a pronoun.

Nominalized verbs are counted in the miscellaneous words category with names and honorifics. They are included in this category because the use of a verb to perform a nominal syntactic function signals that the NP is atypical and marked. Thus, it is not likely to pattern the same way as lexical nouns. As abstract concepts, all the nominalized verbs in the text are either referential-definite (as are proper nouns and honorifics) or generic. In terms of cognition, proper nouns and honorifics are entries in the permanent memory of those who share them as unique referents. Consequently, proper nouns and honorifics are given information. Whether referential-definite or generic, nominalized verbs share with proper nouns and honorifics the characteristic of being given information.

For step two of phase three, I considered classifiers as a potential device for marking topics. In this discussion, I follow Givón (1984a) in considering grammatical roles (subject, object, etc.) as grammaticalized topics. Using the same text from step one, I identified the primary and secondary topics and the case roles of the referents within the sixty-six clauses in *A Broken Sword*. To determine the primary and secondary topics of the clauses, I used the criteria discussed in Givón (1984a:135–85, 1990:739–78) and Shibatani (1991), which are presented below in (36)–(38). Vietnamese grammar, like the grammars of other languages, typically codes one to three levels of topicality within a single clause (36).

(36) SUBJECT>DIRECT OBJECT>OTHERS

I used the topic hierarchy shown in (37) for identifying the primary and secondary topics and applied the topic hierarchy parameters to the data in a particular sequence (38).

(37) AGT>DAT/BEN>PAT>LOC>INSTR/ASSOC>MANNER

Methodology

(38) a. If the simple clause has an **agent** argument, it will be the subject.
b. If the simple clause has no agent but has a **dative/benefactive** argument, it will be the subject.
c. If the simple clause has no agent, nor dative/benefactive but has a **patient** argument, it will be the subject.
d. Etc.

Based on these criteria, the primary topic of a clause is the argument whose case role has the highest place on the topic hierarchy, and the secondary topic is the argument whose case role has the second highest place on the topic hierarchy. The statistics for the primary and secondary clausal topics (hereafter called subjects and objects, following Givón 1983, 1984) are grouped in separate tables and include the number of times each referential strategy is used as either a subject or object. When a clause has more than two arguments, these remaining NPs are grouped with the objects. At this point in the analysis, the distribution of classified NPs is compared with the distribution of the five other categories of reference (kin terms, pronouns, nouns, zero anaphora, and the names-verbs-honorifics category) with the purpose of identifying which referential strategy is used most frequently to refer to subjects. Among the subjects are the most topical and thematic referents in a text. Thus, classifiers can be ranked with regard to the frequency of their use in referring to the most important salient referents in the narrative.

The most thematic referents in a narrative are by definition the most continuous: they persist in the discourse with the same case role for a number of clauses. If classifiers code the most salient or thematically important referents, this is likely to be reflected in the number of continuous topics with which they are used. After grouping the subjects and objects in separate lists, I identified the referents which are continuous or discontinuous topics, and noted the referential strategy used. The statistics in one list include the total number of times each type of referential strategy occurs as continuous or discontinuous subjects, and the statistics for the other list include the number of times each type of referential strategy occurs as continuous or discontinuous objects. When analyzing the NPs in terms of referential continuity, I treated elliptical mentions as units in a sequence of continuous reference. For example, when one or more elliptical mention follows an explicit reference and the next explicit NP is the same referent in the same case role, I labeled the second explicit referent continuous. Similarly, when one or more elliptical mention follows an explicit reference and the next explicit NP is a different referent, I labeled the second explicit referent discontinuous.

For these statistics, the NPs are subdivided into two additional groups in terms of their use or nonuse in coding main or peripheral characters in the narrative. The seven most frequent referents are considered main characters, and the rest are considered peripheral. Referents are deemed main or peripheral characters based on the overall frequency (OF) of the referents and an intuitive interpretation of the story as a whole, so the OF measurement must be completed before one proceeds with this step. In this study, I presented the results from the OF measurement with the results from the analysis of the referential distance (RD) and referential persistence (RP) measurements because, like RD and RP, OF focuses on the thematic importance of referents. OF identifies certain referents as more or less thematically important relative to the other referents, and RD and RP measures referents' levels of thematic importance. While the procedures in step three also provide information about the thematic importance of referents, the purpose of step three is to determine the type of NPs with which classifiers tend to be used, and whether or not classifiers are used to mark subjects or objects.

For steps three and four of the discourse analysis phase, the OF, RD, and RP measurements are applied to the same text used in steps one and two. The OF of a referent is simply the number of times a referent appears in an entire text. The figure includes every reference to a particular entity, regardless of syntactic category. For example, in *A Broken Sword*, *nó* 'it [arrogant]', *mãng x* 'python', *miệng con qu i vật* 'mouth of the monster', *đuôi* 'tail' (of the python), and *đấu* 'head' (of the python) are all considered references to the python as a thematic character. The more thematically important a referent is, the higher its OF. The most thematically important referents in the narrative are the referents with the highest OF relative to the other referents in the text. Any referent that is mentioned three or more times should be considered as potentially important. In *A Broken Sword*, seven referents occur at least five times more than all the other referents, and are main participants in the action of the story. Therefore, these seven referents were considered the main characters, and all the other referents were considered peripheral characters. After identifying the main characters in *A Broken Sword*, I divided their OF figures into explicit NPs and zero anaphora. The higher the OF percentage of anaphora, the more continuous a referent is. The more continuous a referent is, the more important it is. I also calculated the percentage of classifier NPs in each referent's OF, ignoring distinctions between anaphoric or nonanaphoric classifier use. Then, I compared the ratios to each other. As markers of referential salience,

Methodology

the percentage of classifier NPs in a more thematically important referent's OF should be higher than the percentage of classifier NPs in a less thematically important referent's OF.

In step four of the discourse analysis phase, referential distance (RD) and referential persistence (RP) measurements are applied to the NPs in the data. The RP considers the referent in its immediately proceeding context, and the RD considers the referent in its immediately preceding context. The RP figure leads to conclusions concerning a referent's importance. That is, the higher the number, the more persistently mentioned the referent is, and the more persistently mentioned the referent is, the more likely it is that the referent is thematically important. To find a referent's RP, one counts the number of mentions of the referent which occur within the ten subsequent clauses. As with the OF, every reference to a participant is counted, regardless of the syntactic category used.

One measures the RD by finding the last previous mention of the referent and counting the number of clauses between that mention and the current mention. The lower the RD, the more continuous the referent, and the more thematically important it is. I set the maximum number for the RD at twenty, after Givón (1983, 1990). (That upper limit was set arbitrarily in the sense that the twentieth previous clause does not have a specific significance compared to the twenty-first or nineteenth previous clause.) I also assigned the RD 'twenty' to all initial mentions of a referent. When determining the RD for the NPs in *A Broken Sword*, I did not formally consider interference, or the potential ambiguity from referents of similar semantic class. That is, I did only an informal calculation of the number of other referents intervening between the antecedent and its anaphor. The instances of interference were insignificant in terms of quantity and in terms of the referents affected. The majority of NPs which had interference were thematically insignificant based on OF; therefore, I chose not to include this information with the other results.

In both the RP and RD figures, elliptical mentions were included. For instance, if a referent is mentioned three times by zero anaphora and two times by explicit reference—all in the ten subsequent clauses—the RP of the referent is five. In terms of the RD, if an elliptical anaphor occurs three clauses before the referent being measured, and an explicit anaphor occurs four clauses before the same referent, the referent's RD is three.

When another mention (whether explicit or elliptical) of the referent being measured occurs within the same clause, the mention is included in the RP or RD. When this happens with regard to the RP, the mention is counted only if it occurs after the referent being measured. When this happens with regard to the RD, the mention is counted only if it precedes the referent being measured. In such a case, the RD has a value of one.

A referent in metonymous relationship to its antecedent was counted as an explicit mention of the antecedent, but not vice versa. For example, in (39) 'tail' refers back to the python, so is counted in the RP of 'python'. Conversely, 'python' is not counted in the RD of 'tail', since the whole ('python') is not equivalent to one specific part ('tail').

(39) Sword:37, 38

Măng	**x**	đau	qu	k u	rống	l n
python snake	be^suffering	go^beyond	cry^out	bellow	go^up
[AJ]	N	[SV]	V	V	V	[V]

rồi	quật	**đuôi**	tới	tấp	khiến	người	thanh	ni n	ngã
then	whip	tail	advance	<	cause	person	youth	<	tumble
N	V	N	[V]	<	V	GC	N>	<	V

lăn	đi	mấy	vòng.
roll	go	some	circle
V	V	IDN	N

The deeply suffering **python** cried out then whipped its **tail**, fast and thick, causing the youth to tumble in circles.

Similarly, in instances in which the antecedent is collective, dual, or plural, and has a singular anaphor, the anaphor is counted in the antecedent's RP, but the antecedent is not counted in the anaphor's RD. An example of this case is the singular anaphor 'husband' and its dual antecedent 'married couple' in (40)–(41). The RP for 'married couple' includes 'husband', but the RD for 'husband' does not include the dual unit 'married couple'; the RD for 'husband' is not one clause. The RD for 'husband' is the number assigned to all initial mentions, i.e., twenty.

(40) Mosquito:1

Ng y	xưa	tại	một	ngôi	l ng	nhỏ	có	**hai**	**vợ**
day	past	be^at	one	house	village	small	exist	two	wife
GC	[AJ]	[SV]	NU	[MC]	GC	[AJ]	V	NU	N

chồng	trẻ	sống	trong	một	căn	nh	chật
husband	young	be^alive	within	one	house	dwelling	cramped
N	[AJ]	[SV]	[PRE]	NU	[GC]	N	[AJ]

h p.
narrow
[AJ]

Once upon a time in a small village there lived a **young couple** in a shabby house.

(41) Mosquito:2

Người	*chồng*	rất	tốt.
person	husband	very	good
GC	N	[AV]	[AJ]

The **husband** was very good.

With regard to dialogue portions of the text, RD and RP measurements are applied according to the methodology of Givón (1983). When one is counting a referent's RD, if the next previous mention of a referent is in quote material, one counts up to that clause for the RD value. However, if the referent does not appear in a clause of quoted dialogue, one does not count the clause as part of the gap between the referent and its next previous anaphor. Relative clauses are treated the same as quote material; quote material is considered part of the clause that introduces it. For example, in (42) 'he said' is the main clause.

(42) He said, "Give me that book now!"

For the RP counts, both quote material and relative clauses were ignored. All other types of clauses were treated as main clauses.

3.5. Cross-linguistic comparison. The final phase of the study consisted of two parts, discussion of the findings from a study of the anaphoric use of classifiers in Japanese (Downing 1986), and application of the principles used for distinguishing the function of classifiers in White Hmong (Riddle 1989) to the Vietnamese data. Downing's investigation of the anaphoric use of classifiers in Japanese is pertinent to this study in that it presents several classifier functions (use of classifiers for initial mentions and in pronominal reference) that can be identified or discounted through the quantitative distribution analysis I employed for earlier sections of this study.

In the final phase of analysis, I presented an example of classifier use in White Hmong discourse from Riddle and compared it with a Vietnamese discourse example from the data for this study. Riddle apparently uses what Givón (1990:908) calls "conscious and verbal measures" to gauge the importance of classified versus nonclassified NPs. While I used text frequency measures for most of this study, in 4.14 I also applied four principles used by Riddle. The first guideline is that classifier use depends on the semantics of the classifier and the other words in the immediate context. In other words, one must choose a classifier whose meaning is appropriate for the entity to which it refers. For example, a speaker would not use *quả* 'small, roundish object' to classify a wall. Guideline two states that given information is more likely than new information to require a classifier. Consequently, one must assess the NPs in a passage to determine whether or not the referent that potentially needs a classifier is given or new information. Guidelines three and four for classifier use are the need to emphasize a referent as a salient individual and the speaker's judgment about that requirement. These two factors imply that the use of a classifier with a particular referent depends on the relation between the referent and the discourse context, and the subjective view of the speaker. In order to apply the third guideline, one must intuitively assess the level of thematic importance of the referent in question with regard to the storyline. Despite differing methodologies, our studies produce similar observations.

4
Results

The findings of this study support the following analysis of the structure and function of the Vietnamese classifier system. First, numeral classifier constructions in Vietnamese for the most part do not conform to the prototypical syntactic construction for numeral classifiers, and the distribution of classifiers in Vietnamese for the most part does not coincide with the distribution of numbers. Consequently, prototypical syntactic patterns do not come close to explaining the classifier system in Vietnamese. Second, despite its deviation from the traditional, sentence-level norm, Vietnamese shares some characteristics with other classifier languages, and these similarities help in understanding the Vietnamese classifier system better. With regard to discourse, similarities between the Japanese and Vietnamese classifier systems shed light on two classifier functions—anaphoric reference and marking initial mentions. Similarities between the White Hmong and Vietnamese classifier systems are found in the individuation and salience functions, also with regard to discourse. Third, the discourse context provides a perspective which allows one to observe functions of Vietnamese classifiers not apparent in smaller contexts. An explanation associated with discourse features in the language can account for classifier use in a way that an explanation associated with a syntactic or a semantic function does not.

4.1–4.3 Numbers

4.1. Prototypical numeral classifier constructions. By the definition of prototype, the prototypical classifier construction for a given numeral classifier language is likely to occur more frequently than other classifier constructions found in the language. In Vietnamese, the prototypical classifier construction is number + classifier + noun, such as the NP in (43), where MC is a modifying classifier. In the four texts used in this study, however, there are few examples of this classic configuration compared with the number of other classified and nonclassified NPs. Only 36 of the 714 NPs in the data conform to the prototypical syntactic numeral classifier construction for Vietnamese.

(43) Mission:10

đem	ba	con	trâu	đực
bring	three	animal	buffalo	male
V	NU	MC	N	AJ

...bring **three male buffaloes**

Greenberg (1977:278) addresses this discrepancy, stating that some numeral classifier languages have a large group of nouns which do not necessarily need to be classified. Dixon (1986:106) agrees that this situation is not unusual; classifier languages almost always have some nouns which do not take a classifier. In the data for this study, 64% (464) of the 714 NPs contain neither a number nor a classifier, as for example the five NPs in (44), below.

(44) Mission:8

Ông	liền	cõi	ngựa	về	triều-đing	tâu
gentleman	immediately	ride	horse	return	royal^court	address
KIN	[V]	V	N	[V]	N	V

lại	với	Vua	về	cậu	bé	nh	qu
again	toward	king	about	3s	young	dwelling	countryside
[AV]	[PRE]	N	CJ	KIN	AJ	N	N

Results 51

đó
that
DM

He immediately rode his **horse** back to the **royal palace** and addressed the **king** again regarding **that young country boy.**

Given this situation, perhaps the prototypical construction occurs solely among numeral or classified NPs. However, according to the figures for this study, 86% (219) of the 255 NPs that contain a number, classifier, or both also deviate from the prototypical pattern. For example, in (45) a number occurs with a noun but no classifier, and in (46) a number appears with a classifier but no noun.

(45) Mission:34

v	ra	lệnh	năm	tới	phải	sản	xuất	th m
and	go^out	decree	year	arrive	must	produce	go^out	more
CJ	V	N	GC	[V]	MD	V	V	[V]

ch n trâu	con
nine buffalo	offspring
NU N	[GC]

...and ordered (our village) to produce **nine** more **buffaloes.**

(46) Mission:11

cho	chúng	để	th m	ch n	con	nữa
for	[PLURAL^person]	give^birth^to	more	nine	offspring	more
CJ	PRO	V	[V]	NU	[GC]	AV

v o	năm	tới
enter	year	arrive
[V]	GC	[V]

...in order to produce **nine young buffaloes** next year.

As indicated by the statistics in (47) and (48), only 15% of the classified NPs in the four Vietnamese texts conform to the prototypical phrase level syntactic pattern for numeral classifiers. Moreover, only 10% of the NPs in the four texts contain a number, while 33% of the NPs contain a classifier.

(47) Numeral and classifier NPs in the four texts

Text name	NPs	NPs which contain a number		NPs which are prototypical numeral classifier NPs		NPs which contain a classifier		NPs which contain a number and a classifier	
Sword	203	17	8%	7	3%	83	41%	12	6%
Mission	155	21	14%	14	9%	66	43%	18	12%
Tinh	208	16	8%	6	3%	50	24%	13	6%
Mosquito	148	19	13%	9	6%	40	27%	14	9%
Total	714	73	10%	36	5%	239	33%	57	8%

(48) Tally of numeral NPs

Text name	numeral NPs	numeral NPs which are prototypical numeral classifier NPs		numeral NPs which contain a classifier	
Sword	17	7	41%	12	71%
Mission	21	14	67%	19	90%
Tinh	16	6	38%	12	75%
Mosquito	19	9	47%	14	74%
Total	73	36	49%	57	78%

While a substantial percentage (78%) of numeral NPs in the data are also classified NPs, and 49% of the numeral NPs in the four texts consist of the prototypical number + classifier + noun construction, a mere 24% of the classified NPs contain a number. These figures suggest that in Vietnamese, the use of a classifier with a number is a tendency rather than a syntactic requirement. Moreover, while a number tends to require the use of a classifier, the use of a classifier does not require the use of a number. Given these statistics, the presence of a number cannot in and of itself account for classifier use.

4.2. The significance of higher and lower numbers in the data. The frequency of higher and lower numbers in the data indicates that lower numbers are used much more often than higher numbers. Of the eight different numbers which appear in the four texts, the five numbers under twenty account for almost 95% of all the numeral NPs. The chart in (49) shows a summary of small and large number use in the data.

Results

(49) Higher and lower numbers in the data

Text name	NPs with numbers 1–20		NPs with numbers 20+		classifier NPs, numbers 1–20	classifier NPs, numbers 20+
Sword	17	100%	—		12	0
Mission	21	100%	—		18	0
Tinh	11	73%	4	27%	7	5
Mosquito	19	100%	—		14	0
Total	68	95%	4	5%	51	5

A tally of the numeral NPs in the four texts is shown in (50) by construction type. The figures for the prototypical numeral classifier construction are listed in bold type.

(50) Tally of numbers in the four texts by syntactic construction

Construction Type	Number 1	2	3	9	18	100	1,000	10,000	Total #1–9	Totals for all #s
Text: Mission										
# + N / kin	2		1						3	3
# + CL + N	8	1	5						14	14
# + CL	2	1		1					4	4
Total	12	2	5	2	0	0	0	0	21	21
Text: Mosquito										
# + N / kin	4	1							5	5
# + CL + N	6	3							9	9
# + CL + CL	1								1	1
# + CL	3	1							4	4
Total	14	5	0	0	0	0	0	0	19	19
Text: Sword										
# + N / kin	5								5	5
# + CL + N	7								7	7
# + CL	2	1	1		1				4	5
Total	14	1	1	0	1	0	0	0	16	17
Text: Tinh										
# + N / kin		2^{15}	2						4	4
# + CL + N	1	1					2	2	2	6
# + CL	4	1				1			5	6
Total	7	4	0	0	0	1	2	2	11	16
Totals for all texts	47	12	6	2	1	1	2	2	67	73

The statistics show that 100% of the prototypical numeral classifier constructions contain the number one, two, or three. This trend is not surprising, since 89% of numeral NPs in the data contain one of these numbers, and 49% of numeral NPs conform to the prototypical pattern. For the other numbers in the data, the number of occurrences is insufficient to illustrate a significant trend in their distribution.

---

[15] The NP counted in this category consists of the construction number + kin + classifier-noun. The classifier-noun is a compound form, but is not adjacent to the numeral. Therefore, the NP fits the number + noun / kin pattern. Because the compound contains a classifier, I also count the NP in the tallies for classified NPs.

Results   55

4.3. Numbers functioning as non-numbers. Observations about the use of each number in the data are likely to shed light on the relation between number and classifier use. Given that the numbers one, two, and three appear in 89% of all the number constructions and 67% of the classified numeral constructions in the texts, evidence regarding the use of these numbers should be especially telling.

A surprisingly low percentage of numbers in the texts function as numbers. In the seventy-three numeral NPs in the data, only thirty, or 41%, of the numbers function as numbers. In the remaining forty-three numeral NPs, the numbers function either idiomatically or as indefinite articles; note (51)–(52).

(51) Tally of numbers 1–3 by use in the four texts

		Mission	Mosquito	Sword	Tinh	Total, all texts
	number	5	3	1	4	13
1	indefinite article	6	10	11	3	30
	compound or idiom	1	1	2	0	4
2	number	2	4	—	2	8
	compound or idiom	—	1	1	2	4
3	number	5	—	—	—	5
	compound or idiom	—	—	1	—	1

(52) Tally of numbers above 3 in the four texts

	Mission	Mosquito	Sword	Tinh	Total, all texts
9 number	2	—	—	—	2
18 number	—	—	1	—	1
100 number	—	—	—	1	1
1,000 compound or idiom	—	—	—	2	2
10,000 compound or idiom	—	—	—	2	2
Total, all numbers in (50)–(51)	21	19	17	16	73

As the statistics in tables (51)–(53) show, almost 65% of all numeral constructions involve the number one. Moreover, in well over half the NPs in which it appears (64%), the number one marks indefiniteness; it indicates indefiniteness 23% more often than it specifies a quantity of one, and 36% more often than it is used in idioms. In fact, 41% of all the numeral constructions in the four texts involve the number one functioning as an indefinite article.

(53) Distribution of use of 'one' in the data

Use of 'one' as	among 'one' constructions		among numeral NPs	among all the NPs
number	13	28%	18%	2%
indefinite	30	64%	41%	4%
compound or idiom	4	8%	5%	.5%
all uses of 'one'	47	100%	64%	6.5%

The number one differs from other numbers not only because it functions as an indefinite article, but also because it appears frequently in both classified and nonclassified NPs; it appears in 61% of the classified numeral NPs and in 76% of the nonclassified numeral NPs; see (50) in §4.2. This distribution is important because if classifiers are indeed associated with definiteness, as it has been posited,[16] classified NPs which are indefinite should be marked differently from classified NPs which are definite. For example, indefinite classified NPs may involve 'one' used as an indefinite article, and definite classified NPs may not contain 'one'.

4.4–4.6 Definiteness

4.4. Definiteness and indefiniteness. As mentioned previously, some linguists have suggested that classifiers mark definiteness in Vietnamese. "*Definite* denotes a grammatical category which expresses unique reference, where unique reference is the presupposition on the part of the speaker that the hearer is able to identify the intended referent uniquely on the basis of previous knowledge or the situational context" (Dyvik 1983:24). Since Vietnamese is a morphologically uninflected language, one might expect the language to represent definiteness in the syntax via function words, such as the definite and indefinite articles in English, 'the' and 'a'. Examples such as (54)–(55) could be used to show the definite-indefinite distinction, in which a classifier (in this case a GC) marks a definite referent, and 'one' without a classifier indicates an indefinite referent.

---

[16]Stroganov 1974; Adams, Conklin, and Becker 1975.

(54) Sword:21

người	**con**	**g i**	lau	nước	mắt
person	offspring	girl	wipe	liquid	eye
GC	KIN	N	V	N	N

The girl dried her tears.

(55) Sword:18

cậu	thấy	**một**	**cô**		**g i**	xinh	d p
3s	perceive	one/a	young^woman		girl	be^cute	be^beautiful
KIN	V	NU	KIN		N	[SV]	[SV]

He saw **a beautiful girl**.

However, some NPs introduced by *một* 'one' contain a classifier even though a classifier is a potential marker for definiteness and 'one' often marks indefiniteness. In (56) the NP containing the classifier *con* 'animal' is marked for indefiniteness by *một* 'one', resulting in 'a (MC) python'.

(56) Sword:1

ng y	xưa	tr n	vùng	núi	no	có	**một**
day	past	on/upon	region	mountain	other	exist	one/a
GC	[AJ]	RN	N	N	DM	V	NU

con	mãng	x
animal	boa	snake
MC	N	N

Once upon a time in another mountain region there was **a python**.

A classified NP may be indefinite even though it is syntactically unmarked for this distinction, that is, when *một* 'one' is absent from the NP, as in 'a (KCL) young man' in (57). Thus, in Vietnamese an NP's status with regard to definiteness does not appear to be consistently marked by either a classifier or *một* 'one' (cf. (54) and (58)). The NP 'high mountain' in (57) also contains no marking of the NP's definiteness.

(57) Sword:9

thời	bấy	giờ	có	ch ng	thanh ni n	được	một
time	then	time	exist	young^man	youth	[PASSIVE]	one/a
N	N	GC	V	KCL	N> <	ASP	NU

nh	sư	nuôi	dường	ở	một
respected	Buddhist^monk	rear	support	be^located^at	one/a
GC	N	V	V	[SV]	NU

ngôi	chùa	tr n	núi	cao
temple	temple	on/upon	mountain	be^high
MC	N	RN	N	[SV]

At that time, there was **a young man** who had been raised by a monk in a pagoda on **a high mountain**.

In some instances, definiteness does not need to be marked because it is clear that the hearer recognizes the referent as either given information or unimportant information. Example (58) shows two NPs without syntactic marking for definiteness, where the two NPs *rừng* 'forest' and *suối* 'stream' are thematically insignificant. Note that the NPs are unclassified and do not contain the indefinite *một* 'one'.

(58) Sword:43, 44

giết	được	mãng x	rồi	ch ng	kh t
kill	finish^successfully	boa snake	then	young^man	be^thirsty
V	ASP	N N	N	KCL	[SV]

nước	qua,	bỏ	chạy	v o	rừng	tìm	suối	giải
liquid	go^beyond	leave	run	enter	forest	seek	stream	quench
N	V	V	V	[V]	N	V	N	V

kh t
thirst
[SV]

Having killed the python, **the young man** was excessively thirsty, so ran off into **the forest** to find **a stream** to quench his thirst.

Results 59

Many NPs which contain a classifier are definite, as in *ch ng* 'young man' in (58), but many NPs which do not have a classifier are also definite, as is *núi* 'mountain' in (59). Since *núi* 'mountain' was introduced three clauses earlier (57), it is given information and the speaker is sure that the hearer can uniquely identify this referent. Although *núi* 'mountain' is definite in (59), the speaker chose not to use a classifier. In addition to being given information, as with *rừng* 'forest' and *suối* 'stream' in (58), *núi* 'mountain' is an unimportant referent.

(59) Sword:12

v	cho	phép	xuống	núi
and	give	permission	go^down	mountain
CJ	V	N	V	N

...and gave him permission to descend **the mountain**.

While classifiers in Vietnamese appear in indefinite as well as definite NPs, they appear in far fewer indefinite NPs than definite NPs. This is not surprising, since definite references occur with a higher frequency, whether classified or nonclassified. The statistics from *A Broken Sword* in (60) bear out the prominence of definite NPs. With regard to indefiniteness, the statistics indicate that almost one-third of indefinite NPs in the text contain *một* 'one'. Moreover, the majority of indefinite NPs that are classified contain *một* 'one', and all of the NPs that contain both a classifier and *một* are indefinite.

(60) Definiteness of NPs in *A Broken Sword*

	Generic or Generic Plural	Definite NPs	Indefinite NPs	all NPs
Classifier NPs	3 4% of 83 20% of 15	60 72% of 83 40% of 151	20 24% of 83 54% of 37	83 41% of 203
Classifier NPs with *một* 'one'	—	—	10 100% of 10 27% of 37	10 5% of 203
all NPs	15 7% of 203	151 74% of 203	37 18% of 203	203

While *một* 'one' appears in both classified and nonclassified NPs, it appears in definite NPs only as part of a compound or idiom. Even when *một* 'one' is used as a number, a classifier may be absent from the NP, as in example (61), in which the numeral NP 'one wish' lacks a classifier. In Vietnamese, then, *một* usually implies a NP is indefinite, and does not require a classifier. Conversely, however, the use of a classifier does not imply a NP is definite, and does not necessarily need *một* to mark the NP when the NP is indefinite.

(61) Mosquito:20

dạ	thưa	con	chỉ	xin	**một**
[courteous]	reply^politely	[your^child]	only/just	request	one/a
FW	PRT	KIN	PRT	V	NU

điều
pretext
N

Sir, I have only **one wish**.

4.5. Classifiers as markers of initial mentions. Classified NPs in Japanese, Malay, and Burmese are often used for initial mentions of referents, and this may also be a classifier function in Vietnamese. However, percentages of initial and post-initial mentions in one Vietnamese narrative (*A Broken Sword*) indicate that this is not likely: 43% of the initial mentions in the text contain a classifier, and 57% do not contain a classifier. Among post-initial mentions, 40% contain classifiers, and over 60% do not contain a classifier.

A classified, indefinite initial NP may even be used for the same referent later as a definite NP, as is *ch ng thanh ni n* 'a young man' in (62), and 'the young man' in (63). The fact that classifiers are used for both definite and indefinite, initial and post-initial mentions confirms that the classifier is an unlikely candidate for either a marker of definiteness or of initial mentions.

(62) Sword:9

thời	bấy	giờ	có	**ch ng**	**thanh ni n**	
time	then	time	exist	young^man	youth	<
N	N	CAT	V	KCL	N>	<

At that time…there was a young man…

Results 61

(63) Sword:13

tr n	đường	về l ng	qu	**ch ng**
on/upon	road	to native^village	countryside	young^man
RN	N	[V] CAT	N	KCL

thanh ni n
youth <
N   <

On the way back to [his] native village, the young man...

With regard to the definiteness of initial mentions, we see that in *A Broken Sword*, nouns are used as often as classifier NPs to introduce new referents. While the evidence in (64) shows that both classifiers and nouns are used for new mentions, it does not give a clue as to why a Vietnamese speaker chooses one over the other strategy of referring.

(64) Definiteness of initial mentions in *A Broken Sword*

Type of NP	Classifier NPs	Nouns	All Other NPs	Total
Definite	11	11	5	27
Indefinite	17	12	2	31
Generic or generic plural	3	9	2	14
Total	31	32	9	72

The evidence examined—the prototypical numeral classifier construction, the co-occurrence of a classifier with numbers and the indefinite marker *một* 'one', and classifiers in initial and post-initial mentions—would seem to suggest that any connection between definiteness and classifiers in Vietnamese is coincidental.

4.6. Classifiers and anaphoric reference. According to Thompson (1965:148), the general categorical (GC) is the most common class of substantive used for anaphoric reference, where anaphoric reference denotes "reference back to a person, time, or place which has just been mentioned or somehow otherwise called to attention." Further, while GCs may syntactically stand alone the way a noun or pronoun can, modifying classifiers (MCs) may not appear this way. Contrary to these syntactic parameters, the data for this study show that both GCs and MCs may be used anaphorically; the two specifier subtypes are not in complementary distribution based on syntax. This is seen in examples (65)–(68).

(65) Mission:17 (antecedent)

xin	giao	cho	ch u		một	**con**	trâu	v
request	entrust	to	young^relative		one	animal	buffalo	and
V	V	PRT	KIN		NU	**MC**	N	CJ

một bao gạo
one bag rice
NU GC N

Please give me **one buffalo** and one bag of rice.

(66) Mission:18 (anaphor)

hai	**con**	còn	lại	thì	đem	l m	thịt	v	nấu
two	animal	remain	moreover	then	take	make	meat	and	boil
NU	**MC**	V	[AV]	PRT	V	V	N	CJ	V

hai	bao	gạo	co	cả		l ng		ăn	nhậu
two	bag	rice	for	all/the^whole		village		eat	booze
NU	GC	N	CJ	PRT		GC		V	V

Please have **the other two** killed for meat and cook the two bags of rice for our whole village to enjoy.

(67) Mission:3 (antecedent)

một	vị		cố-vấn	nh		vua	đi	ngang	qua	c nh
one	revered^one		advisor	respected		king	go	across	by	field
NU	[GC]		N	[GC]		N	V	[V]	CJ	N

đồng	thấy	một	**người**	đ n		ông			v
tree	perceive	one	person	[HONORIFIC]		male^relative			and
N	V	NU	GC	KIN		KIN			CJ

Results

đứa	*con*	*trai*
[lower^rank]	offspring	young^man
MC	GC	N

One of the king's counselors happened to pass by a rice field and saw **a poor man and his son**.

(68) Mission:36 (anaphor)

ta	*ch*	*muốn*	*thử*	*c c*	***người***	*m*	*thôi*
1s	just	want	try	various	person	but	only/just
PRO	PRT	V	V	PL	**GC**	PRT	PRT

I just wanted to test **you all**.

Nevertheless, the data do show that MCs are used much more frequently as classifying-type entities than as pronouns, and GCs are used as pronouns more often than MCs are used that way; see (69)–(71). The MC versus GC distinction thus is evident within the discourse environment, but only weakly. Unfortunately, this single distributional variation between the two syntactically-based subtypes does not substantiate Thompson's claim that MCs and GCs comprise separate grammatical categories.

(69) Summary of pronominal use of MCs and GCs[17]

	Used as pronoun		Not used as pronoun		Total	
MCs	3	6% of 50	47	94% of 50	50	17% of 296
		3% of 102		24% of 194		
GCs	99	40% of 246	147	60% of 246	246	83% of 296
		97% of 102		76% of 194		
Total MC and GC	102	34% of 296	194	66% of 296	296	

---

[17]The slight discrepancy among figures in tables (18), (69), (71), and (127) amounts to less than 1% variation and does not affect the conclusions of this research.

(70) Tally of pronominal use of MCs and GCs by text

	Sword	Mission	Tinh	Mosquito	Total
MC as pronoun	1	2	0	0	3
GC as pronoun	15	24	26	34	99
Total	16	26	26	34	102
% pronominal use of MCs and GCs in the texts	17%	33%	44%	52%	34%

As a subtype of GC, kin classifiers might be expected to pattern like GCs. However, the statistics bear out that a greater percentage of kin classifiers (81%) than GCs (29%) or MCs (6%) are used as pronouns. Given the high percentage of kin classifiers used as pronouns, and their differing semantic domain, the possibility of the kin classifier as a separate grammatical category or specifier subtype should be considered. The chart in (71) is a summary of kin classifier use in relation to GCs. (The use of kin classifiers is discussed in 4.18.)

(71) Percentage of pronominal use of GCs and KCLs

	Used as pronoun		Not used as pronoun		Total
Non-kin classifier GCs	55	29% of 192 56% of 99	137	71% of 192 93% of 147	192
KCLs	44	81% of 54 44% of 99	10	19% of 54 7% of 147	54
GCs and KCLs	99	40% of 246	147	60% of 246	246

4.7–4.8 Distribution of classifiers compared to other strategies of referring

4.7. Strategies of referring in Vietnamese. The categories used for referents in Vietnamese include honorifics and kin terms, as well as the grammatical categories of nouns, pronouns, zero anaphora, and classifiers. The frequency of classifier NPs compared to the frequency of other categories used for referring in *A Broken Sword* is listed in (72).

Results

(72) Tally of explicit and zero anaphora NPs in *A Broken Sword*

	1 Classifier	2 Kin term	3 Pronoun	4 Noun	5 Proper nouns, verbs, honorifics	6 Zero anaphora	7 All NPs
#NPs	70	15	11	41	15	40	192
% (excluding zero anaphora)	46%	10%	7%	27%	10%	—	100%
% (including zero anaphora)	36%	8%	6%	21%	8%	21%	100%

According to these statistics, the most preferred form of reference is the classifier construction (used 36% of the time). Among explicit forms of reference, the second most preferred strategy of referring is the noun phrase, but among all strategies of referring, the second most preferred category includes both noun phrases and zero anaphora, each type being used 21% of the time. The frequency with which these three referential categories are used implies that they carry a higher functional load than the other forms. However, the statistics indicate neither the function nor the distribution of these forms. To determine the functions of the most preferred reference strategies, one must observe their distribution in discourse. In 4.8, I examined statistics based on that distribution.

4.8. Distribution of classifiers with regard to referent continuity.
Overall patterns of distribution for each strategy of referring reveal that particular forms are used in specific environments. A referent's relative level of importance within a local context is the principal characteristic which a speaker takes into account (albeit subconsciously) when choosing forms of reference in discourse. The NPs in the text were grouped according to their use as continuous or discontinuous topics, because this binary distinction divides mentions in terms of more and less thematically important mentions. The more continuously a referent is mentioned, the more thematic it is compared to the other referents in local contexts, i.e., episodes.

In terms of topicality, the NPs in the text are further divided by primary clausal topics and secondary clausal topics. Primary clausal topics (hereafter termed subjects, following Givón) represent the most active participants in a story. Since they represent topical referents, they represent the most thematically important participants in a narrative. Therefore, one would expect that more subject NPs are members of the continuous category than of the discontinuous category. Indeed, of the ninety-two subject NPs in *A Broken Sword*, 59% are continuous and 41% are discontinuous; see (73).

Based on the statistics in (73), it appears that a Vietnamese speaker prefers zero anaphora over the other referential forms when referring to continuous subjects, using zero anaphora 63% of the time. Consistent with this preference, 94% of all the subjects represented by zero anaphora in *A Broken Sword* refer to continuous referents, and 6% refer to discontinuous referents. When a mention is discontinuous, however, a Vietnamese speaker is more likely to use a classifier construction than any other strategy of referring. Classifier constructions are used for discontinuous subjects more than twice as frequently as for continuous subjects.

(73) Primary clausal topics (subjects) in *A Broken Sword*

	Continuous topic		Discontinuous topic		Total	
Classifier construction	11	32% 20% of 54	23	68% 61% of 38	34	37% of 92
Kin term	5	62.5% 9% of 54	3	37.5% 8% of 38	8	9% of 92
Pronoun	3	60% 6% of 54	2	40% 5% of 38	5	5% of 92
Noun	—	0% 0% of 54	2	100% 5% of 38	2	2% of 92
Proper nouns, verbs, honorifics	1	14% 2% of 54	6	86% 16% of 38	7	8% of 92
Zero anaphora	34	94% 63% of 54	2	6% 5% of 38	36	39% of 92
Total	54	59% of 92	38	41% of 92	92	

In terms of main versus peripheral characters in the text, over 94% of zero anaphor subject NPs refer to main characters, and 63% of the continuous mentions of main-character subjects occur as zero anaphora; see

(74). These statistics confirm the speaker's preference for zero anaphora over other strategies when referring to continuous, main-character referents. The distribution of classifiers confirms that their function is also primarily associated with marking thematically important referents. Ninety-one percent of classified subject NPs refer to main characters. In addition to referring to main characters, classifiers are used to mark discontinuous mentions. Sixty-eight percent of the classified NPs referring to subject main-characters are discontinuous mentions, and 62% of the discontinuous mentions of main-character subjects occur as classifier constructions. While a few discontinuous, main-character NPs are marked by the other strategies of referring, no nouns are used for this purpose. Given these statistics, the joint status of a referent as a main-character subject and a discontinuous mention constitutes a strong conditioning environment for classifier constructions.

(74) Main versus peripheral subjects in *A Broken Sword*

	Continuous topic		Discontinuous topic		Total
	Main	Peripheral	Main	Peripheral	
Classifier construction	10 29% 20% of 51	1 3% 33% of 3	21 62% 62% of 34	2 6% 50% of 4	34 37% of 92
Kin term	5 62.5% 10% of 51	0 — %	3 37.5% 9% of 34	0 — %	8 9% of 92
Pronoun	3 60% 6% of 51	0 — %	2 40% 6% of 34	0 — %	5 5% of 92
Noun	0 — %	0 — %	0 — %	2 100% 50% of 4	2 2% of 92
Proper nouns, verbs, honorifics	1 14% 1% of 51	0 — %	6 86% 17% of 34	0 — %	7 8% of 92
Zero anaphora	32 89% 63% of 51	2 5.5% 67% of 3	2 5.5% 6% of 34	0 — %	36 39% of 92
Total	51 55% of 92	3 3% of 92	34 37% of 92	4 5% of 92	92

Although peripheral character mentions comprise less than 10% of all the primary clausal topics, they nonetheless comprise 37% of all the mentions in the text; cf. (74) and (76). Unfortunately, since their distribution does not neatly complement the patterns of the other referential forms observed thus far, the distribution of peripheral characters among subject NPs in *A Broken Sword* poses a minor dilemma; see (74). By definition, a peripheral character is less important than a main character. Despite the fact that the less important a character is in the narrative and thus the lower its continuity in the text, four of the nine peripheral character subject NPs fall under the continuous topic category. Admittedly, their membership in the continuous category does not necessarily indicate that their continuity, and therefore, their thematic importance, is high. Their status as continuous mentions only implies their continuity is higher relative to other referents in local contexts. However, if my observations regarding zero anaphora and classifier constructions are correct, their membership in those categories should suggest that they are actually main characters. Adjusting the hypothesis, I can resolve the dilemma by equating the zero anaphor and classifier categories to refer to the general group "thematically important referents relative to the other referents in the local context" instead of to the group "main characters defined in terms of the text as a whole."

Turning now to the continuous, main-character category, one-third of classified subjects (a surprisingly substantial portion) are continuous mentions. This gives rise to the question: "Why does such a high percentage (29%) of classifier constructions mark this presumed zero anaphor category?" Of the eleven tokens in this category, two are occurrences of the classifier *nh* 'respected', which refers to a king or a Buddhist monk. There is no evidence to dispute the status of *nh* as a genuine classifier for either referent. A third token is the occurrence of *của* 'possession' in reference to the 'python's temple'. All eight remaining tokens in this category occur as the kin classifier *ch ng* 'young man'. This referent is the main character in the narrative, so there is no doubt as to its thematic importance. Six of the eight classified tokens occur along with ten continuous zero anaphora tokens referring to *ch ng* during the central conflict in the story (between clauses 29 and 45). The two remaining tokens occur in a single clause at another climactic point in the story (clause 55). However, according to the statistics analyzed thus far, classifier constructions normally mark discontinuous mentions. This kin classifier's eight occurrences in the continuous mentions category could indicate that kin classifiers have a different discourse function than other types of classifiers. Note that semantically speaking, *nh* is not a kin classifier, but a title. A speaker uses *nh* to talk about a king or Buddhist monk, but not to address them, whereas a speaker uses kin classifiers both in talking about and to the referent named by the classifier (Thompson 1965:294–303).[18] With so few tokens in the data for either referent classified by *nh* , a comparison of their distribution with that of *ch ng* 'young man' leaves this issue inconclusive.

Coupled with the understanding of the distribution of subject NPs in the text, the distribution of object NPs, shown in (75), adds to the perspective of the relationship between classifier constructions and the other strategies of referring. (I use "objects" to refer to secondary and tertiary clausal topics, following Givón 1984.)

(75) Primary clausal topics (objects) in *A Broken Sword*

	Continuous		Discontinuous		Total
Classifier construction	—	0%	36	100% 38% of 96	36
Kin term	1	14%	6	86% 6% of 96	7
Pronoun	1	17%	5	83% 5% of 96	6
Noun	1	3%	38	97% 40% of 96	39
Proper nouns, verbs, honorifics	1	12.5%	7	87.5% 7% of 96	8
Zero anaphora	—	0%	4	100% 4% of 96	4
Total	4		96		100

As the statistics thus far show, more subjects tend to be continuous, and thus more thematically important, than discontinuous. Furthermore, compared to subject case roles, object case roles represent referents of lesser importance in the immediate context. Given this situation, it is not surprising that a much higher percentage of subject NPs (59%) than object NPs (4%) are continuous mentions. Likewise, it is not surprising that among the object NPs no continuous mentions are marked by a classifier construction or a zero anaphor. The two categories are used principally to imply the higher thematic importance of a

---

[18]For examples of the use of *chàng* and *nhà*, see *A Broken Sword*, clauses 27, 29, 56–58, and §4.18.

referent relative to the other referents in the context. However, it is surprising that classifier constructions mark 38% of discontinuous-mention objects, and nouns mark only 2% more discontinuous objects than classifier constructions; see (75). Given that objects represent less thematic referents, one might expect far more of them to be expressed as nouns than as classified constructions. However, when the main and peripheral character distinctions are taken into account, the distributional patterns of two of the categories overlap to an even greater extent, as seen in (76). In terms of main and peripheral objects in *A Broken Sword*, 61% of classified, discontinuous objects and 69% of the nominal, discontinuous objects are peripheral characters. This distribution of classifier constructions diverges from the pattern among classified subjects.

(76) Main versus peripheral objects in *A Broken Sword*

	Continuous topic		Discontinuous topic		
	Main	Peripheral	Main	Peripheral	Total
Classifier construction	0 — %	0 — %	14 39% 34% of 41	22 61% 40% of 55	36
Kin term	1 14% 33% of 3	0 — %	5 71% 12% of 41	1 14% 2% of 55	7
Pronoun	1 17% 33% of 3	0 — %	4 67% 10% of 41	1 17% 2% of 55	6
Noun	1 3% 33% of 3	0 — %	11 28% 27% of 41	27 69% 49% of 55	39
Proper nouns, verbs, honorifics	0 — %	1 12.5% 100% of 1	5 62.5% 12% of 41	2 25% 3.5% of 55	8
Zero anaphora	0 — %	0 — %	2 50% 5% of 41	2 50% 3.5% of 55	4
Total	3	1	41	55	100

Taking into account the gradience of thematicity, it is possible that the reason for the distribution of main and peripheral objects in the noun and classifier referential categories is that classifier constructions mark peripheral characters which are more thematically important to the storyline than those marked by nouns. Indeed, the average case role (96) of the twenty-seven discontinuous, peripheral-character, noun objects is lower on the topic accession hierarchy than the arguments marked by other referential strategies in the same clause (Givón 1984:139, and ff).[19] That is, when ranking the arguments based on case roles, the object that has the highest case role on the topic hierarchy is the most likely to become a continuous topic; in a clause with two or more objects, this object is consistently classified. The average case role for classified objects in this category is 1.18. Cross-linguistically, one of the ways that initial mentions of important referents tend to be coded in classifier languages is by the use of a classifier. Among these two categories of discontinuous peripheral character objects, the percentage of initial mentions is higher for classified NPs (82%) than for object NPs (74%).

Reviewing the conclusions reached thus far, it is apparent that the distribution of classifier constructions among subject-mentions suggests that the factor determining the speaker's choice of a classifier construction over other strategies of referring is the status of the referent as main (more thematically important) rather than peripheral (less thematically important). The distribution of classifiers among subjects also leads one to conclude that classifier constructions are the normal marking for discontinuous mentions. Zero anaphora for the most part refers to continuous, main-character subjects. The distribution of referential strategies among objects highlights the use of classifier constructions for discontinuous mentions which are more likely to become continuous, i.e., important, topics than those referred to by noun phrases. Consequently, based on their use in discourse, zero anaphora, noun phrases, and classifier constructions are roughly in complementary distribution.

4.9–4.10 Referent importance and referent continuity

4.9. Overall frequency. One of three textual measurements used in this study which reflect the topic importance of referents within a narrative is overall frequency (OF). The frequency with which the referents occur throughout *A Broken Sword* is directly related to their thematic importance; see (77)–(78). If zero anaphora and classifier constructions

---

[19] I assigned a value of 1 to the primary clausal topic, a 2 to a topic in the same clause which had the next highest place on the topic accession hierarchy, and so on. Then, I added these values for object-nouns in the discontinuous, peripheral-character category in order to calculate the average case role value, repeating the process for classified objects.

mark the most thematically important referents, the figures should show that the more thematically important the referent, the higher the percentage of zero anaphora and classifier NPs in its OF.

Thirteen referents in *A Broken Sword* are mentioned three or more times as shown in (77). Seven referents have OFs of five or higher, and thus, are the most thematically significant referents in the narrative.

(77) Overall frequency of referents in *A Broken Sword*

Referent	Overall # of tokens		Referent (cont.)	Overall # of tokens
young man	56	58	Buddhist monk	4
young man's hand and foot	2			
			citizens	3
python	26	33		
python's head and tail	7		a maiden	3
king		19	girl's mother	3
girl		19	princess	3
python's temple		14	wedding	3
patrolman	11	13		
patrolman's face	2			
sword	5	10		
sword fragment	5			

(78) Overall frequency of thematic referents in *A Broken Sword*

Reference strategy	young man, his hand, foot	python and python's head, tail	king	girl	python's temple	patrolman and face	sword and fragment
# tokens zero anaphora	20	5	7	2	1	4	2
# tokens marked reference	38	28	12	17	13	9	8
Total: 163	58	33	19	19	14	13	10
% of referent's reference which is zero anaphora	34%	15%	37%	10.5%	7%	31%	20%

Results 73

Considering only marked reference, the ranking of these seven referents, from most to least thematically important, is: the young man, the python, the girl, the python's temple, the king, the patrolman, and the sword. This ranking corresponds to an intuitive understanding of the narrative; that is, a reader giving his or her subjective interpretation would agree with such a ranking.

Based on the OF figures which include both implicit and explicit reference, the high OF of the young man, the python, the girl, and the king distinguish them as the most thematically important of the seven referents represented in (78). The percentages of zero anaphora use also distinguish particular referents as more or less important than the other referents. However, the OF figures and the zero anaphora percentages do not exactly coincide with each other. Based on zero anaphora, the three main (or most continuous) referents are the young man, the king, and the patrolman, instead of the young man, the python, and the girl (or the king).

(79) Distribution of classifier NPs for thematic referents

# and % of NPs	young man, his hand, foot	python and python's head, tail	king	girl	python's temple	patrolman and face	sword and fragment
# of classified NPs	26	9	4	1	4	5	7
% of classified reference	45%	27%	21%	5%	29%	38%	70%

The frequency percentages of classifier NPs associated with each of the seven referents are also inconsistent with the frequency percentages with regard to zero anaphora, as shown in (79). Frequency percentages of classifier NPs rank the young man, the sword, and the patrolman as the three main characters. These statistics suggest that neither the percentage of classifier NPs nor that of zero anaphor NPs used for a referent in a narrative coincides with a clear ranking of more or less thematically important referents, as assessed by OF. While the OF measurement can be effectively used to distinguish the few most thematically important referents in the text, it cannot be used to correlate the thematic importance of referents with the referential strategies used to code them.

4.10. Referential distance and referential persistence. The average referential distance (RD) and referential persistence (RP) for referents in *A Broken Sword* reflect the same trends evident in the distribution of referents with regard to referent continuity (4.8). Considering the average RD for subject NPs, the NPs marked as zero anaphora have the lowest values, as expected; see (80). These NPs are the most continuous in terms of lookback; the lower the RD value, the fewer the number of clauses (on the average) between the referent and its most recent previous mention. The high RD (5.26) for classifiers reflects the large percentage of classifier constructions used for discontinuous topics; other referents in the same case role tend to intervene between one classified NP and the next. The average RD values of the remaining four categories also reflect the distribution patterns found in 4.8, although the number of tokens in each of these categories is low (less than eight). For example, the second lowest RD average belongs to kin terms. Since all the subject NPs represented by kin terms are main characters, 62.5% of which are continuous topics, the low RD is expected (this percentage is taken from (73) in 4.8). The miscellaneous category, column 5 in (80), contains proper nouns and honorific terms. It is likely that the miscellaneous category has an RD value between those of the kin term and noun categories because honorific terms are semantically similar to kin terms, and proper nouns are similar to nouns.

(80) Average RD and RP for subject NPs in *A Broken Sword*

	1 Classifier	2 Kin term	3 Pronoun	4 Noun	5 Proper nouns, verbs, honorifics	6 Zero anaphora	7 All subject NPs
RD	5.26	1.25	1.2	19.5	4.57	1	3.28
RP	5.15	4.38	3.8	2	3.86	4.89	4.72

The RP figures for the subject NPs present no unexpected patterns. The figures confirm that zero anaphora (RP 4.89) tends to mark subjects of higher topic persistence relative to the other referents in the narrative. Likewise, the figures confirm that classifiers mark topics which are referentially persistent; the referents marked by classifiers in the subject case role are the most highly persistent referents in the text, with an average of five occurrences of the same referent in the ten subsequent clauses. Kin terms, pronouns, and miscellaneous nouns are all less persistent than classified and zero anaphora NPs, and nouns have the lowest persistence of all the strategies of referring.

When I compared the RD and RP averages for all the subject NPs with those of all the object NPs, I again found no surprises, column 7 in (80)–(81). The subject NPs in *A Broken Sword* have the low average RD value of 3.28, while the object NPs have the high average of 13.07. Subjects have a markedly lower RD value than that of objects because they are much more continuous than objects. By definition, a subject is mentioned more often and is more important than an object. Consequently, subjects have a higher persistence value (RP 4.72) than that of objects (1.18) because they tend to persist in discourse while objects do not.

(81) Average RD and RP for object NPs in *A Broken Sword*

	1 Classifier	2 Kin term	3 Pronoun	4 Noun	5 Proper nouns, verbs, honorifics	6 Zero anaphora	7 All subject NPs
RD	14.53	7.29	1	16.59	4.63	10.75	13.07
RP	.94	5	2.33	.15	2.38	2.5	1.18

Like the RD and RP figures for subjects, the figures in (81) for objects also confirm my previous findings related to referent continuity. Few objects are continuous or persistent. In particular, classified objects are consistently discontinuous, with an average of over fourteen clauses between its use and the last previous mention of the same referent. In terms of the subsequent discourse, unlike classified subjects, they do not tend to persist. Classified objects are not even mentioned once on the average in the ten succeeding clauses. The RD and RP values for nominal and classified objects provide evidence that classified objects are more thematic than nominal objects. The RD for both nouns and classifiers is extremely high, and the RP for both categories is extremely low. However, the RD for classifiers is slightly lower than that of nouns; thus, classified NPs are slightly more continuous than unclassified nouns. Likewise, the RP for classifiers is slightly higher than that of nouns; thus, classified NPs are slightly more persistent than nouns.

The noticeably high RD average for zero anaphora objects (10.75) reflects the use of zero anaphora for marking unimportant objects or impersonal expressions. For example, the bracketed object [them] in the free translation of example (82) is an elliptical mention in Vietnamese. Because this elliptical object occurs only once in the text, it has an RD of 20 and an RP of 0 (zero). An RD value of 20 signifies the low continuity of the referent, and the RP value of 0 signifies the nonpersistence of the referent.

(82) Sword:6

> Vua   thấy   vậy phải sai   dựng một ngôi đền   cho
> king perceive so must command build one temple temple for
> N   V   DM MD   V   V   NU   [MC]   N   CJ
>
> nó   ở
> 3s^ARROG live
> PRO   V

The king, perceiving this, had to order **them** to build a temple for it to live in.

The figures presented in this section confirm that a Vietnamese speaker tends to use a classifier with a referent of higher thematic importance, whether presenting the referent in the subject or object case role. A classified subject is typically a new or reintroduced topic, but is mentioned more persistently than other subjects in the subsequent discourse. Also typically discontinuous are classified objects, which have a much higher average RD than classified subjects. Both classified and nominal objects represent discontinuous mentions and tend not to persist in the discourse. The difference between classified and nominal objects resides in the relative importance of the referent. While the referents represented by both classified and nominal objects are of the lowest thematic importance compared with those represented by other strategies of referring, classified NPs mark referents that are more important than those marked by nouns.

Although these figures show that a speaker uses classifier constructions to mark the more thematically important referent relative to other referents in the discourse, the more detailed scope of this function is still unclear. For example, there are entire clauses and sentences which do not contain a single classifier. The passage in (83)–(85) is just one example of this phenomenon.

(83) Sword:30

> Nói xong, **người** thanh ni n   d n   cô   g i
> talk finish person   youth <   lead   young^woman   girl
> V   V   GC   N>   <   V   KIN   N

ra	khỏ	đền	
out^from	escape	temple	
V	V	N	

Having finished talking, **the youth** led the young woman out of the temple.

(84) Sword:31

rồi	trở	v o	cầm	kiếm	trong	tay	s n
then	return	enter	take^hold^of	foil	within	hand	be^ready^to
[AV]	[V]	[V]	V	[N]	[PRE]	N	[SV]

s ng	chờ	mãng	x	trở	về.
<	await	boa	snake	return	return
<	V	N	N	[V]	[V]

…then came back in, taking the foil in hand, ready to await the python's return.

(85) Sword:32

V o	khoảng	nửa	đ m,	ch ng	bỗng	nghe
about	<	midnight	<	young^man	suddenly	hear
[V]	[GC]	N	GC	KCL	AV	V

tiếng	cây	cối	g y	răng	rắc	ngo i	cổng
sound	tree	[shrubbery]	be^broken	crack	<	outside	gate
GC	[GC]	N	[SV]	N	[V]	RN	N

đền.
temple
N

At about midnight, the **young man** suddenly heard the **sound of twigs** snapping outside the temple gate.

Clause 31 contains no classifiers, but is bounded by clauses which contain at least one classified NP each. Preceding clause 31 is clause 30, which contains the classified NP *người thanh ni n* 'youth'. Following clause 31 is clause 32, with the kin classifier *ch ng* 'young man' and the classified NP *tiếng cây cối g y răng rắc* 'sound of twigs snapping'. One might posit that because the primary clausal topic *người thanh niên* 'youth' in clause 30 is classified and the primary clausal topic in clause 31 is the same referent represented by a zero anaphor, no classifier is necessary in clause 31. While this explanation is possible, it does not explain why two classified NPs are used in clause 32. In the next section I examine referential salience as the explanation for this dilemma.

4.11–4.12 Cross-linguistic comparison of classifier functions

4.11. Anaphoric use of classifiers in Japanese compared to Vietnamese.

The discourse use of classifiers in another Asian classifier language—Japanese—may offer a clue to the role of numeral classifiers in Vietnamese discourse. The numeral classifier system of Vietnamese shares similarities with the system of Japanese. The two languages are similar in several ways: classifiers in Japanese and Vietnamese appear in contexts similar to explicit pronouns; both languages reflect the linguistic influence of Mandarin (another numeral classifier language in Asia); and both languages have a well-developed system of honorifics.[20] Classifiers in Japanese can be used for initial mentions, and referents introduced by classifiers are relatively more important than other referents. Despite the noted similarities, at least some of the differences between Japanese and Vietnamese lie in the functions of their numeral classifier systems. For example, while nonhuman classifiers are rarely, if ever, used as pronouns in Japanese (Downing 1986), both human and nonhuman classifiers are used as pronouns in Vietnamese. Of the 296 classifiers used in the texts for this study, 49% (145) refer to humans, and 51% (151) refer to nonhumans. Examples (86)–(87) show a nonhuman classifier used pronominally, and examples (88)–(89) show a human classifier used pronominally.

(86) Mission:17

xin	giao	cho	chú		một	con	trâu
request	entrust	for	[young^REL]		one	animal	buffalo
V	V	PRT	KIN		NU	MC	N

Please give me **one buffalo**.

---

[20]The assumption behind considering honorifics as a pertinent similarity is that the system of expressing familial and social relationships influences the referential system.

(87) Mission:18

hai	**con**	còn	lại	thì	đem
two	animal	remain	moreover	then	take
NU	MC	[AV]	[AV]	PRT	V

Take **the other two**

(88) Mission:5

nhưng	**đứa**	con	trai	của
but/yet	[lower^rank]	offspring	young^man	possession
CJ	MC	GC	N	GC

ông	không	phải	nghĩ	ngợi	lâu
male^relative	not	must	ponder	<	long^while
KIN	NG	MD	V	<	N

But his **son** did not have to think long.

(89) Mission:10

người	hãy	đem	ba	con	trâu	đực	v	ba
person	be^sure^to	take	three	animal	buffalo	male	and	three
GC	MD	V	NU	MC	N	[AJ]	CJ	NU

bao	gạo	tới	l ng	**đứa**	bé	đó
bag	rice	to	village	[lower^rank]	small	there
GC	N	[V]	GC	MC	[AJ]	DM

Take three male buffaloes and three bags of rice to **that boy's** village.

Another difference between the use of anaphoric classifiers in Japanese and Vietnamese lies in the speaker's motivation for choosing a classifier instead of another anaphoric form. In Japanese, the choice of reference is a more distinct dichotomy between implicit and explicit reference than the choice in Vietnamese. A Japanese speaker tends to use implicit reference (a zero anaphor) for post-initial mentions of a main character, and explicit reference (a classifier construction, a noun phrase) for post-initial mentions of a peripheral character. Implicit reference is used even when explicit mention of another character makes the reference ambiguous; that is, zero anaphora is often used even when the character is a discontinuous topic. The reason behind this phenomenon is related to the referential strategies Japanese speakers use in narrative. Clancy (1980:131–133), in comparing the referential choices of English speakers with Japanese speakers, shows that third person pronouns are absent from the references chosen by Japanese speakers in the twenty narratives studied. That is, Japanese speakers tend to use two referential strategies almost exclusively: either zero anaphora (73% of the references counted) or noun phrases (27%).

Conversely, a Vietnamese speaker tends to use elliptical references less than half as often (21%) as a range of explicit references; see (71) in 4.7. Further, the data support a dichotomy not between implicit and explicit reference, but rather between zero anaphora and classifier constructions, given particular conditions. Since particular conditions (e.g., discontinuous mention of the referent which marks it as important) tend to be required for the use of classifier constructions, there are in Vietnamese narrative, unlike in Japanese narrative, commonly used middle forms of reference between noun phrases and ellipsis.

In summary, the anaphoric use of classifiers in Vietnamese is similar to the usage in Japanese in few ways. Like classifiers in Japanese, classifiers in Vietnamese can be used for initial mentions; however, as the statistics from this study indicate, more classifiers are used for post-initial mentions than for initial mentions. Like classifiers in Japanese, classifiers in Vietnamese can be used pronominally; however, while only human classifiers may be used pronominally in Japanese, both human and nonhuman classifiers are used pronominally in Vietnamese.

4.12. Referential salience in White Hmong compared to Vietnamese. White Hmong, like Vietnamese, has been influenced by languages of the Sino-Tibetan, Tai, and Austroasiatic families because speakers of White Hmong, like those of Vietnamese, live in areas bordering on these linguistic areas. Given this similarity, the classifier system of White Hmong is likely to be more similar to that of Vietnamese than the classifier system of Japanese is. White Hmong shares with Vietnamese a diversity of semantic and syntactic classifier properties. Classifiers in White Hmong are said to be required with numerals, quantifiers, and demonstratives; with possessive NPs; with question words requiring a definite or numeral response, and in some nominalized forms. One semantic function which has been recognized in both White Hmong and Vietnamese is individuation. Individuation can be thought of as an aspect of multiplicity; instead of emphasizing quantity, as when a classifier appears with a number, the classifier without a number

Results 81

emphasizes singularity. However, according to Riddle (1989), in White Hmong the classifier emphasizes singularity not in the same sense as it does with the number one. Rather, a classifier without a number individuates the referent which its NP represents. It says, syntactically, that this particular referent is important.

In discourse in White Hmong, the semantic function of individuation correlates with referential salience. Salient refers to that which is "conspicuously noticeable; projecting or pointing outward" (Flexner and Hauck 1987:791). White Hmong uses classifiers to individuate, or to direct the hearer's attention to a particular focus. Speakers indicate the higher salience of one referent relative to the other referents in the local context by marking the most salient NP with a classifier. In the White Hmong example (90) from Riddle 1989:11, only one of the four occurrences of *teb chaws* 'country' is classified. In (90a) *teb chaws* represents the initial mention of 'country', and since the focus at this point in the discourse is on the action of war breaking out, it is unclassified. In (90b) and (90c), in addition to the emphasis again being on the action rather than the place, the classifier that would be used for *teb chaws* 'country' clashes semantically with the action. The classifier for *teb chaws* would conflict with the focus of fleeing or leaving the country because it normally classifies 'container-like objects and places with boundaries'. However, in (90d), the classifier for *teb chaws* is used and emphasizes the action of staying in the country.

(90) a. *peb   tau   tawg   rog   nyob rau **teb   chaws** los   tsuas*
       we   [past] break war   stay in   country <   Laos   <

   We had war break out in **Laos.**

   b. *Vaj   Pov   tau   khiav tawm **teb   chaws***
      Vang Pao [PAST] run   leave country <

   Vang Pao left the **country.**

   c. *neeg   kuj   txhua leej   txhua tus   tsuas nrhiav   kev*
      person then   all   person all   CL   only   look^for way

      *tawm   **teb   chaws**   los   tsuas   tuaj   mus   rau   sab*
      leave   country <   Laos   <   come   go   to   side

thaib teb.
Thailand

Everyone looked for a way to leave **Laos** and go to the Thai side.

d. *Kuv tau peb   hnub tomqab xav   hais tias yog tsis khiav*
   I   get three day   after   think that < if   not run

*ces   yuav nyob **lub teb**   **chaws los**   **tsuas** ntawd*
then will stay CL country <   Laos <   there

Three days after that I thought that if I didn't escape, then I would live in **Laos**...

    Riddle (1989) concludes that four major factors condition the use of a classifier in White Hmong: the semantics of the classifier and the other words in the immediate environment; the status of the information as given or new; the need to emphasize a referent as a salient individual; and the speaker's judgment on that need. The pragmatic function which synthesizes all four factors is referential salience.

    Similarly, in Vietnamese, speakers indicate the higher topical importance of one referent relative to the other referents in the text by marking the most important NP with a classifier. When classifier NPs in Vietnamese are tracked by their distribution in the text, one condition becomes clear: classifiers consistently identify thematically significant referents over nonthematically significant referents. An example of this classifier function can be seen in an excerpt from a narrative, examples (91)–(94).

(91) Sword:46

Ng y hôm   sau,   một vi n   l nh   tuần
day afternoon place^behind one official patrolman patrol
GC   GC   RN   NU   [GC]   N   V

đi ngang qua ngôi   đền.
go across <   temple temple
V [SV]   <   [MC]   N

The next day a patrolman came across the temple.

Results 83

(92) Sword:47

Hắn	vô		cùng	ngạc		nhi n	thấy		**mãng**
3s	extremely	<		be^surprised		so	perceive		boa
PRO	[SV]		N	V		CJ	V		N

x	nằm	chết	tr n	vũng	m u,	còn	cô	
snake	be^lying	die	on	puddle	blood	remain	young^woman	
N	[SV]	V	RN	[GC]	N	[V]	KIN	

g i	thì	biến	đâu	mất.
girl	then	vanish	where?	be^lost
N	PRT	V	DM	[SV]

He was extremely surprised to see the **python** lying dead in a puddle of blood, the young woman vanished.

(93) Sword:48

Nhớ	tới	lời	hứa	của		nh	vua,	hắn
remember	to	promise	<	possession		respected	king	3s
V	[V]	GC		V	GC	[GC]	N	PRO

lập	tức	x ch	**đầu**	**mãng**	x	về	cung
immediately	<	carry	head	boa	snake	return	palace
V	[GC]	V	N	N	N	[V]	N

xin	lãnh	thưởng.
request	receive	reward
V	V	N

Remembering the king's promise, he immediately carried the **python's head** back to the palace to get the reward.

(94) Sword:49

Thấy	**đầu**	con	**mãng**	x ,	nh	vua	mừng	rỡ
perceive	head	animal	boa	snake	respected	king	exult	<
V	N	MC	N	N	[GC]	N	[SV]	<

hỏi
ask
V

Seeing the **python's head**, the exultant king asked...

The same four factors used for the White Hmong example can be used in interpreting the Vietnamese examples in (91)–(94). By considering the semantics of the words used, the status of information, and the speaker's judgment on a referent's salience, it is seen that the classifiers in this Vietnamese example follow the patterns of the White Hmong classifier system. The python *mãng x* in (92) is not classified the first time the referent appears in the episode; even though the patrolman is seeing the python for the first time, the most salient aspect of the encounter is that the python is dead. Upon seeing the puddle of blood, the patrolman immediately recognizes this. Note that the word for 'puddle' is classified in this clause (92). In clause 48 (93), the patrolman decides to take the python's head to the king to claim a reward. Neither 'head' nor (possessive) 'python' are classified in clause 48 because the emphasis is on the promise *lời hứa của nh vua* (which appears classified) that motivates the patrolman to act. As a result of the patrolman's action, the king sees the python's head. The focus is on the king seeing the python's head, so both 'python' and 'king' are classified (94). While the speaker has the option of using *của* 'possession' to classify the python, s/he chooses to use *con* 'animal'. This classifier precludes any referential ambiguity that might arise in association with the generic body part *đầu* 'head', which can refer to a human as well as an animal. Note that in both clauses 47 and 48 the speaker's judgment on salience overrides the use of a classifier for the python. Furthermore, it is the importance of the action that dictates the use of a classifier for the python's head in clause 49. The choice of which classifier to use appears to be a secondary consideration related to disambiguating the details, while the decision of whether or not to use a classifier is a primary consideration related to illuminating the thematic thread of the narrative.

Reexamining the passage from 4.10 in which a clause with no classifiers is bounded on either side by a clause with classifiers, the absence of classifiers can also be explained by referential salience. The passage is reproduced below, with an additional preceding clause to provide more context, (95)–(98). When the four criteria are used to interpret this second Vietnamese example, several features become evident. First, as seen through the statistics, a speaker does not automatically use a classifier for a referent that is an important thematic referent and discontinuous mention. In clause 29, a sword is reintroduced after its initial introduction eighteen clauses before. The sword plays an important role not only in the succeeding portion, but also in the remainder of the narrative. Although it is an important referent and a discontinuous object in clause 29, the sword is not classified. Instead, the sword appears with the classifier *bao* 'scabbard', indicating the most salient attribute of the clause; the emphasis is on the scabbard being emptied. The young man then emphasizes what came out of the scabbard by using a classifier plus demonstrative adjective to refer to the sword.

(95) Sword:29

Rút	*gươm*	*ra*	*khỏi*	**bao,**	**ch ng**	*nói*
pull^out	sword	came^out	escape	scabbard	young^man	talk
V	N	V	V	GC	KCL	V

tiếp,	*'Đã*		*có*	**c i**	**n y**	*nói*
continue	[to^have^already]		possess	one^thing	this	talk
ASP	ASP		V	MC	DM	V

chuyện	*với*	*nó.'*	*Cô*		*đi*	*mau*
conversation	against	3s^ARROG	young^woman		go	be^quick
N	PRE	PRO	KIN		V	V

đi.
[COMMAND]
ASP

Drawing a sword out of its **scabbard**, the **young man** went on talking: "I have this **thing** to say to it. You must go quickly!"

(96) Sword:30

Nói	*xong,*	**người**	*thanh ni n*		*d n*	*cô*	*g i*
talk	finish	person	youth	<	lead	young^woman	girl
V	V	GC	N>	<	V	KIN	N

```
          ra      khỏ   đền
          out^from escape temple
          V       V     N
```

Having finished talking, the **youth** led the young woman out of the temple,...

(97) Sword:31

```
rồi   trở    v o   cầm           kiếm  trong  tay   s n
then  return enter take^hold^of  foil  within hand  be^ready^to
[AV]  [V]    [V]   V             [N]   [PRE]  N     [SV]

s ng  chờ   mãng x     trở    về.
 <    await boa   snake return return
 <    V     N     N    [V]    [V]
```

...then came back in, taking the foil in hand, ready to await the python's return.

(98) Sword:32

```
V o     khoảng  nửa  đ m,  ch ng       bỗng      nghe tiếng
about   interval half night young^man  suddenly  hear sound
[V]     [GC]    N    GC    KCL         AV        V    GC

cây  cối         g y          răng rắc   ngo i   cổng đền.
tree [shrubbery] be^broken    tooth crack outside gate temple
[GC] N           [SV]         N    [V]   RN      N    N
```

At about midnight, the **young man** suddenly heard the **sound of twigs** snapping outside the temple gate.

Clause 32 illustrates the second feature of classifier use in this passage. Aside from the young man in clause 30, after clause 29 the next important focus does not appear until clause 32, which begins a new episode. Until this point in the story the python has only been talked about; now, the antagonist itself is heard through the ears of the hero. With the sound of breaking shrubbery, the python's appearance looms imminent. For emphasis, the classifiers in clause 32 point the reader's attention to the python's approach. A classifier, like any word that denotes an appropriate attribute, may be used to refer to a character metaphorically. For example, a speaker might choose to refer to a bearded tour guide as 'the beard up front'. In such a case, 'beard' could be classified. Sometimes, as in clause 32, the classifier itself denotes the item or attribute that refers to the referent. In this instance, *tiếng cây cối g y răng rắc* 'sound (of) twigs snapping' represents the python's approach. Whether the NP consists of a classifier used as a pronoun or a classifier plus other substantives, the classifier not only represents the referent, it also highlights the referent's salience.

An example of individuation is illustrated in clause 30; this is the third feature of classifier use in this passage. Because the young man, as hero, remains salient throughout the narrative, the authors refer to him using the kin classifier *ch ng* 'young man' from the time he is introduced to the end of the story. The Vietnamese authors use the kin classifier pronominally as the default reference strategy for the hero. When the authors want to draw closer attention to the young man, they use the kin classifier as (modifying) classifier, or they use another classifier construction. An example of this use appears in clause 30 example (96), where the young man is referred to as *người thanh ni n* 'young man', literally 'person youth'. In this instance, the classifier *người* 'person' individuates the concept of youth, i.e., it specifies 'one unit of youth', and at the same time emphasizes the young man as the most important argument. Consequently, the classifier in clause 30 functions in terms of both semantic individuation and discourse-level referential salience. This is a divergence from the use of classifiers in White Hmong. Whereas in White Hmong, individuation is reflected as referential salience in discourse, by this example we see that in Vietnamese, the individuation and referential salience functions operate simultaneously and distinctly in discourse.

Having observed the use of several classifiers in clauses 29, 30, and 32, turn now to the absence of classifiers in clause 31. This distribution can be explained by the lack of significant new information in clause 31. In clause 29, the authors underscore the sword as important and emphasize the young man's readiness to use it. Clause 31 also describes the sword and the young man preparing to use it on the python. This information is presented a second time, with no emphasis on a particular part. All these propositions (the location of the young man, the foil in his hand, his preparation for the python, and the python's return) provide a setting for the action that follows. Although the story's main character is the semantic agent of this clause packed with this setting or background information, syntactically he remains in the background himself, without explicit marking of an agent; the hero is referred to in clause 31 only by zero anaphora. While salient, new information requires the use of a classifier, old, background information is marked by the absence of classifiers.

In the preceding examples, the subjective side of the referential salience function of classifiers is illustrated. In using classifiers, a speaker has the option to emphasize particular referents, to individuate particular concepts, and to express a referent metaphorically and classify it as thematically significant at the same time.

Given that White Hmong and Vietnamese have long shared the influence and features of the same language families (Sino-Tibetan, Tai, and Austroasiatic), it is not surprising that the classifier systems of the two languages pattern similarly. In both systems, classifiers are used in local contexts to individuate arguments on the basis of quantity or quality, and to disambiguate arguments in terms of semantic and syntactic relationship. In extended discourse, the two systems also have a similar comprehensive function. Classifiers identify the most thematically important propositions. Because of this broad function, classifiers in both White Hmong and Vietnamese seem to cross functional boundaries; the functional distribution of classifiers overlaps with such discursive phenomena as pronominal reference, new referent identification, and discontinuous or continuous mentions. Nevertheless, Vietnamese classifiers, like classifiers in White Hmong, can be said to perform a single, basic discourse function: classifiers in both languages signal referential salience.

4.13–4.18 Additional considerations

4.13. Individuation. Individuation is one of the primary semantic functions attributed to classifiers in Vietnamese. This type of individuation differs from the function which Riddle (1989) attributes to classifiers in White Hmong. Her findings suggest that in White Hmong, (semantic) individuation and a discourse function, which she terms referential salience, are the same. However, the findings of the present study show that in Vietnamese, the semantic function of individuation is distinct from the discourse function of classifiers, which I also term referential salience (4.12). In Vietnamese, individuation can be thought of as an aspect of multiplicity; instead of emphasizing quantity, as when a classifier appears with a number, the classifier without a number emphasizes singularity. Vietnamese is said to be a language in which the singular or multiple nature of a referent need not be specified by overt marking in every NP. Stated another way, some constructions in Vietnamese require neither a quantifier nor an individuator. One might use the following example as an

Results 89

explanation for how the individuation function determines the use or non-use of classifiers. In normal human experience one man rides one horse (outside of special circumstances like the circus). A speaker talking about one man riding does not need to specify how many horses the man is riding, as in (99). On the other hand, a man can own any quantity of horses, so if a speaker is talking about the horse or horses a man owns, he must specify the number of horses, as in (100). Based on these examples, one could conclude that for Vietnamese, in the case of the man riding, no classifier is necessary, and in the case of the man owning a horse, a speaker must use a classifier.

(99) Mission:8

Ông	liền	cõi	ngựa	về	tri -đình
gentleman	act^immediately	ride	horse	return	royal^court
KIN	[V]	V	N	[V]	N

He **rode (his) horse** back to the royal palace...

(100) Mission:6

Ng i	có	thể	cho	ch u	biết	con
[his] excellency	possess	may	allow	[young^REL]	know	animal
GC	V	MD	V	KIN	V	MC

ngựa	của	Ng i		đi	được
horse	possession	[his] excellency		go	finish^successfully
N	GC	GC		V	ASP

m y	bước	trong	một	ng y	không	ạ
any^amount^of	step	within	one	day	not	sir/madam
PRO	N	[PRE]	NU	GC	[QW]	[FW]

"Sir, could you please tell us how many steps **your horse** gallops a day?"

However, from the perspective of the discourse context, one can easily refute this analysis. In the deictic situation which precedes (100), the rider, referred to as 'Sir' in (100), sees the ch u 'young relative' with an individual buffalo and asks: "How many furrows can your (MC) buffalo cut in one day?" (appendix B, Mission:3). As with a single man riding a single horse, there is no ambiguity about the number of buffaloes the speaker is referring to, yet the speaker uses a classifier. The boy then replies with a parallel question in (100) for the rider: "Sir, could you please tell us how many steps your (MC) horse gallops a day?" Again, there is no doubt to which horse the boy is referring, yet the speaker uses a classifier. These examples confirm that semantic functions alone (in this case, individuation) do not account for the use of classifiers in Vietnamese.

4.14. Abstractness. While classified NPs can be abstract, they rarely are, because classified NPs must be referential. For example, in Mission: 9 and 14 the words for 'genius', 'strategem', and 'decree' appear without classifiers, but the abstract word for 'vow' in Sword:48 appears with a classifier. Of the eighty-three classified NPs in *A Broken Sword*, only one is abstract.

4.15. Relativization. There was only one example in my data of relativization using the particle *mà* as it is used in Thompson 1965:263 and Nguyễn Đình Hoa 1957:130—to relativize a phrase for a nominal or classified NP. Therefore, I could not compare the constructions in which classifier and nonclassifier NPs were followed by *mà* and a relative clause.

4.16. Marking possession and classifiers. By its use in discourse, *của* 'possession' should be considered a classifier, although few analysts view it as a classifier.[21] There are at least two ways to express that an item belongs to someone, as shown in (101). Option (101a) may be a stylistic variant of option (101b), or *của* may be a classifier used in terms of the NP's relation to discourse.

(101) a.   Sword:15   b.   Sword:22

       đền   của   mãng x   đền   mãng x
       temple possession boa snake   temple boa snake
       N   GC   N   N   N   N   N

       python's temple   python's temple

The word *của* 'possession' is sometimes analyzed as a verb meaning 'belong to' (Thompson 1965:200); however, syntactically *của* appears in constructions similar to those with the classifier *thứ* 'sort' or 'rank'. Both *của mãng x* 'the python's' (101a) and *thứ ba* 'third' (102) function as adjectives modifying the preceding noun.

---
[21]To my knowledge, Thompson 1965 is the only linguist besides myself who views *của* as a classifier.

Results

(102) Sword:40

v	đâm	th m	nh t	**thứ**	**ba**
and	stab	again	stab	order	three
CJ	V	[AV]	N	MC	NU

...and dealt (it) a **third** blow.

A verb meaning 'belong to' does exist in Vietnamese, so a speaker is not limited by lexical set for the concept of possession. A sentence from the story *Son Tinh and Thuy Tinh* illustrates in (103) this alternative to using the word *của*.

(103) Tinh:30

v	thuỷ	cung	tr ng	lệ	sẽ	**thuộc**	**về**
and	water	palace	magnificent	beautiful	shall	belong	belong
CJ	N	N	[AJ]	[AJ]	[MD]	V	V

n ng
damsel
KCL

...and the most magnificent undersea palace will **belong to** her.

These examples illustrate the range of choices a Vietnamese speaker has for expressing possession; to express possession a speaker may choose to use the verb *thuộc về* or word order, but when a classifier is necessary to add referential salience to the possessive concept, a speaker uses *của*. For example, *của* focuses attention on the most significant of two or more referents, as in example 104. The 'python' is the primary focus, marked by a classifier in the first clause. The next important referents in focus are the hero and the third blow to the python, both classified. In (105), in order to highlight the hero and not the hero's sword as the important focus, the classifier *mũi* 'point' must be clearly secondary. The classifier *của* points out the owner of the sword rather than the point of the sword as the important referent. Even though thematically the inanimate sword (in whole or in part) is an extension of the human hero himself, the speaker reemphasizes the human hero by marking him with a classifier because he is more important.

(104) Sword:39, 40

Sắp	bị	lọt	v o	**miệng**	**con**	qu i
be^about^to	[NEG^PASS]	fall^into	enter	mouth	animal	be^odd
[SV]	ASP	V	[V]	N	MC	[SV]

vật	thì	may	thay	**ch ng**	đứng	dậy
creature	then	fortunately	<	young^man	stand^up	wake^up
N	PRT	[SV]	<	KCL	V	V

kịp	v	đâm	th m	nh t	thứ	ba
in^time	and	stab	again	stab	order	three
[AV]	CJ	V	[AV]	N	GC	NU

He was about to fall into the **monster's mouth** when luckily the **young man** stood up in time and stabbed it again a **third stab**.

(105) Sword:41

nhưng	vì	đâm	mạnh	tay	qu	**mũi**	**gươm**
yet	because^of	stab	be^strong	hand	excessive	point	sword
CJ	PRT	V	[SV]	N	[AJ]	[GC]	N

của	**ch ng**	bị	g y
possession	young^man	[NEG^PASS]	be^broken
GC	KCL	ASP	[SV]

But because of the extremely strong-handed stabbing, the **point of the young man's sword** was broken.

Another explanation for the use of *của* 'possession' in example (105) also substantiates *của* as a classifier. Regarding the NP *mũi gươm của ch ng* 'point sword possession young man', perhaps *mũi gươm ch ng* 'point sword young man' would be permissible in terms of sentence grammar. However, in discourse, at times the speaker's meaning may be conveyed by one construction, but not the other. As Vietnamese is uninflected, case roles are unmarked, except by word order. Consequently, they may need clarification when several arguments appear in the same clause. Since the first part of the NP in example (105) contains two arguments ('sword point') and the second part of the same NP contains a third argument ('young man'), the use of *của* 'possession' clarifies any case role ambiguity among the three arguments. The classifier sharpens the listener's focus on the part of the NP which will distinguish the intended meaning from any other interpretation. The most salient or important aspect of the NP is highlighted by the classifier. In example (106), *lời hứa của nh vua* 'promise of the king' could be correctly expressed as *lời hứa nh vua*. However, without *của* 'possession', the NP could also be understood to mean 'promise to the king'. Within the context of the narrative up to this clause, either meaning makes sense. Again, the speaker uses a classifier to disambiguate the case roles.

(106) Sword:48

Nhớ	tới	lời		hứa	của	nh	vua,
remember	to	spoken^words		vow	possession	respected	king
V	[V]	GC		V	GC	[GC]	N

hắn	lập	tức	x ch	đầu	măng	x	về	cung
3s	establish	presently	carry	head	boa	snake	return	palace
PRO	V	[GC]	V	N	N	N	[V]	N

xin	lãnh	thưởng.
request	receive	reward
V	V	N

Remembering the **king's promise**, he immediately carried the python's head back to the palace to get the reward.

As the examples presented here demonstrate, *của* functions the same way other classifiers function in Vietnamese. Thompson and Chappell (1991) suggest that Vietnamese *của* should be analyzed in terms of genitive classification systems. Rather than investigation of a single Vietnamese word in terms of the genitive classification system, I suggest that genitive classification systems be reconsidered with particular attention given to the use of classifiers in discourse.

4.17. Nominalization. Nominalization is said to be a syntactic function of classifiers in Vietnamese. In terms of syntactic relation, nominalization indicates the grammatical set in which to group the information; a nominalized form in effect commands: "treat this as a noun type concept." Among the data there were twenty-nine nominalized forms. In thirteen of those cases a classifier preceded the verb and apparently functioned as the nominalizer. In example (107), *th nh* 'succeed' is nominalized when combined with *t i* 'talent, genius' without a function word. In (108) the classifier *lời* 'spoken words' and the verb *hứa* 'vow' together make a nominalized form, meaning 'promise'. In (109) the verbs *ăn* 'eat' and *ngủ* 'sleep' are understood as nominal concepts without a classifier or other function word.

(107) Sword:11

Sau	*khi*	**th nh**	**t i,**	*nh*	*sư*
place^behind	when	succeed	talent	respected	Buddhist^monk
RN	GC	V	N<	[GC]	N

tặng	*cậu*	*một*	*thanh*	*gươm*	*qúi*
offer	3sg	one	sword	sword	be^noble/precious
V	KIN	NU	[MC]	N	SV

After **graduation**, the monk gave him a special sword...

(108) Sword:48

nhớ	*tới*	*lời*	*hứa*	*của*	*nh*	*vua*
remember	to	spoken^words	vow	possession	respected	king
V	[V]	GC	V	GC	GC	N

Remembering the king's **promise**...

(109) Mosquito:9[22]

v	*sinh*	*ch n*	*nản*	*buồn*	*phiền*
and	give^birth^to	be^tired^of	be^discouraged	sad	worry
CJ	V	[SV]	SV	[SV]	V

đến	*độ*		**mất ăn**	**mất ngủ**	
come^to	measure/time^period		lose eat	lose sleep	
[V]	DM		V V	V V	

...and became so depressed that she could neither eat nor sleep.

---

[22]I analyzed the phrase *mất ăn mất ngủ* 'lose eat lose sleep' as verb + nominalized form + verb + nominalized form in congruence with the example *bắt dầu ăn* 'begin eat' (begin eating), which consists of compound form (verb + noun) + nominalized form, and in contrast with an example such as *không ăn được* 'not eat able' (can't eat), which I analyzed as negative + verb + modality verb (Barker, p.c.).

Results

The chart in (110) lists the tallies of nominalized NPs from the data. Nominalization at the most accounts for only 8% of classifier usage in any one of the four texts, and thus it is clearly not the main function of classifiers. Note also that there were more nominalized forms without a classifier than with a classifier.

(110) Nominalized NPs in the four narratives

	nominalized forms with a classifier	% nominalized forms (among classifiers)	nominalized forms without a classifier	total nominalized forms	% of all NPs which are nominalized
Sword	6	6%	4	10	5%
Mission	1	1%	1	2	1%
Tinh	1	2%	5	6	3%
Mosquito	5	8%	6	11	7%
Total	13	—	16	29	—

Observed in isolation, nominalization makes a non-nominal part of speech nominal. In discourse, nominalization may make a non-nominal part of speech topical. A classifier increases the topic importance of a NP in that a classifier signals that a NP is salient and prominent. As with marking possession, a classifier is an optional part of a nominalized form; a Vietnamese speaker may nominalize a form with or without the use of a classifier. When speakers do use a classifier in a nominalized form, they mark the form as referentially salient.

4.18. Kin term or classifier? The functions of kin terms differ from those of classifiers semantically and syntactically; however, some words share properties with both kin terms and classifiers. These words comprise a subclass which I have called kin classifiers. Kin classifiers share with kin terms the broad semantic domain of referring to humans. The distinction between kin terms and kin classifiers is a subtle one. Kin terms, strictly defined, are those words which denote familial relationship. However, kin terms may be used to refer to and address individuals who are not related by bloodline to the speaker. For example, the kin term *cô* can be used to refer to or address one's paternal aunt, a girl above the age of ten, or a (young) unmarried woman. In (111), *cô* refers to a young, unmarried woman who is unrelated to and a stranger to the man speaking. However, in the case of a kin classifier, the word itself does not connote familial relationship. Thus, speakers do not typically use kin classifiers to refer to blood relatives, while they have the option to do so with kin terms.

(111) Sword:20

Tại	sao	cô	lại	bị
why	how?	young^woman	act^contrary^to^expected	NEG^PASS
INT	DM	KIN	V	ASP

trói	nằm	đây
tie	be^lying^down	be^here
V	[SV]	DM

Why are **you** lying here all tied up?

Speakers also may use a kin term to refer to themselves. For example, in (112) the speaker uses the kin term *em* 'younger sibling' instead of the pronoun *tôi* 'I, my' to refer to herself when conversing with a male stranger who is within the same age range. The word *em* refers to a wide range of individuals, not strictly to a brother or sister in one's immediate family. Note also that the speaker in (112) addresses the stranger using a kin classifier pronominally (*ch ng* 'young man').[23] While speakers may use a kin term to refer to themselves, speakers may not use a kin classifier to refer to themselves.

(112) Sword:27

C m	ơn ch ng,	nhưng	em	không	muốn	ai
thank	< young^man	but	[here^1s]	not	want	anyone
V	< KCL	PRT	KIN	NG	V	IDN

phải	chết	vì	em
must	die	because^of	[here^1s]
MD	V	PRT	KIN

Thank you, but I don't want anyone to have to die because of **me**.

The distinction between human referent classifiers and kin classifiers is perhaps even subtler than the distinction between kin terms and kin

---

[23]This particular kin classifier is restricted to use in literature (Thompson 1965:301; Barker, p.c.).

classifiers. The words in both categories do not refer to blood relations, and the words in both categories emphasize a particular aspect of the human referent. The distinction lies in their semantic domains and their use. The chart in (113) summarizes the domains of use for kin terms, kin classifiers, and human referent classifiers.

(113) Domains of use for the three categories

	Kin term	Kin classifier	Human referent classifier
Reference to familial relationship	yes	no	no
Reference to nonfamilial relationship	yes	yes	yes
Reference to self	yes	no	no
Used in direct address	yes	yes	no
Used in third person address	yes	yes	yes
Used to modify other terms	yes	some	yes
Used pronominally	yes	yes	some

The domains of use that kin classifiers share with kin terms but not with other classifiers may account for the difference in the distribution patterns of kin classifiers and that of other classifiers. Recall from the discussion in 4.6 that many of the classifiers which are used pronominally in the data are kin classifiers. In fact, 43% of all the classifiers used as pronouns in the narratives are kin classifiers; note the chart in (114). Again, although the semantic domains for kin classifiers and other human referent classifiers overlap, their distribution patterns differ. Compared with other human referent classifiers, kin classifiers are used disproportionately as pronouns (81% of the time). Sixty-three percent of the human referent classifiers used as pronouns are kin classifiers, as shown in (115). Consequently, if kin classifiers are separated from the human referent classifier category, less than a third of human referent classifiers would remain in the list of words used pronominally. When kin classifiers are included in that count, almost half of the human referent classifiers fall in the pronominal use category. Thus, the overall distribution pattern of kin classifiers diverges not only from that of all classifiers, but also from that of other human referent classifiers.

(114) Distribution of kin and non-kin classifiers

Syntactic category	Used as pronoun	Not used as pronoun	Total
Kin classifiers	44 81% of 54 43% of 102	10 19% of 54 5% of 194	54 18% of 296
Nonkin classifiers	58 24% of 242 57% of 102	184 76% of 242 95% of 194	242 82% of 296
Kin and nonkin classifiers	102 34% of 296	194 66% of 296	296

(115) Distribution of kin and other human referent classifiers

Syntactic category	Used as pronoun	Not used as pronoun	Total
Kin classifiers	44 81% of 54 63% of 70	10 19% of 54 13% of 75	54 37% of 145
Nonkin, human referent classifiers	26 29% of 91 37% of 70	65 71% of 91 87% of 75	91 63% of 145
Kin and nonkin human referent classifiers	70 48% of 145	75 52% of 145	145

Despite their more prevalent use as pronouns, kin classifiers are also used in environments similar to those of other classifiers. For instance, *ch ng* 'young man' appears in clause 29 of *A Broken Sword* as a pronoun, and in clause 13 as a classifier for *thanh ni n* 'youth' as shown in examples (116)–(117).

(116) Sword:29

Rút	gươm	ra	khỏi	bao,	**ch ng**	nói
pull^out	sword	come^out	escape	scabbard	young^man	talk/tell
V	N	V	V	GC	KCL	V

tiếp
continue
ASP

Drawing a sword out of [its] scabbard, the **young man** went on talking

(117) Sword:13

ch ng	**thanh ni n**	gặp	một	ngôi	đền
young^man	youth <	encounter	one	temple	temple
KCL	N> <	V	NU	[MC]	N

...the **young man** came upon a temple...

As stated in 4.8, kin classifiers are used similarly to kin terms, as both forms of reference and forms of address, while human referent classifiers are used only as forms of reference. Indeed, addressing a person by one of their attributes, such as 'respected' or 'revered', is simply awkward. For example, consider the use of the human referent classifiers *nh* 'respected' and *vị* 'revered' in example (118). The words meaning 'king' and 'advisor' are classified. In every instance of these two classifiers in the data, they classify a noun; they do not occur as pronouns. Five of the nine different non-kin human referent classifiers used in the data have a similar distribution, three of the nine occur as either pronoun or nonpronoun, and one of the nine occurs only as a pronoun. Despite the variation in distribution, as a rule, nonkin human referent classifiers are used solely for reference.[24]

(118) Mission:10

Nh	vua	nói	với	**vị**	cố-vấn
respected	king	tell	toward	revered	advisor
[GC]	N	V	[PRE]	[GC]	N

The **king** told the **advisor**...

While the use of kin terms lies primarily within the semantic scope of blood relations, the use of kin classifiers and nonkin, human referent classifiers lies completely outside that scope. Rather than reflecting any

---

[24]In one instance, one of the nonkin human referent classifiers may be used in direct address; however, more unambiguous evidence is necessary to confirm the term's status as classifier or kin term.

connection between the speaker, addressee, and referent, the kin classifier *ch ng* 'young man' in example (119) identifies the referent in a general sense. In terms of semantics, the nonkin, human referent classifier *người* 'person' classifies the referent in an even more general sense than the kin classifier.

(119) Sword:55

Người	*kh ch*	*lạ*	*n y*	*ch nh*	*l*	***ch ng***	*thanh*
person	visitor	strange	this	precisely	be	young^man	youth
GC	N[lit]	AJ	DM	AV	CP	KCL	N>

ni n	*đã*	*giết*	*con*	*mãng*	*x*
<	to^have^already	kill	animal	boa	snake
<	ASP	V	MC	N	N

This mysterious visitor was precisely the **young man** who had killed the python.

In terms of the discourse context, however, both the kin and the nonkin classifiers in (119) bring the reader's attention to the most important referent and its relevance. In the story, the visitor has just arrived, and the narrator signifies with classifiers that the visitor is a highly significant referent, not a background character.

While the evidence in this study suggests the existence of the subtype kin classifier, other data are needed to substantiate the claim that kin terms also are a type of classifier, as Thompson (1965) posits.

5
Conclusion

5.1. Summary of findings. The principal purpose of this study was to identify the function of classifiers in Vietnamese discourse. The results of this study show that the primary function of the classifier in Vietnamese is not to meet a syntactic requirement set by a number; not to mark definiteness; and not to mark initial mentions. Although classifiers in Vietnamese are found with numbers, in definite NPs, and in NPs of initial mentions, they are also found in contradictory environments: without numbers, in indefinite NPs, and in NPs of continuous referents. Rather, the various syntactic, semantic, and discourse functions previously associated with classifiers, such as nominalization, individuation, occurrence with relative clauses, marking possession or definiteness, and substituting for nouns, can all be seen as consistent with a single, basic discourse function which I term referential salience (after Riddle 1989). By using a classifier, a speaker chooses to call attention to a referent. Consequently, the speaker's choice of classifier is often subjective; this is true both in terms of the local context and overall thematic highlighting. A speaker's use of a classifier also depends on several objective factors. The meaning of a classifier must appropriately correspond to the classified word, and the classifier must be placed appropriately in its syntactic environment.

The fundamental precondition for using a classifier in Vietnamese narrative is that the referent to be classified must be significant to the storyline. The level of significance is continuum-based, is relative to the local discourse context, and is subject to the speaker's judgment. As the statistics in 4.8 show, regardless of whether a referent is continuous or discontinuous, if a referent is higher on the topic hierarchy than the other referents in the clause and is explicitly mentioned, it is with few exceptions classified. The topic importance of a referent dictates whether or not a speaker will use a classifier, and may be measured using OF, RD, and RP. Still, the speaker's reasons for using a classifier in many instances may not be transparent. For example, neither the Buddhist monk nor the wall in (120)–(121) are important based on textual measurements for referent continuity, nor are they important relative to the other referents and events in the story. Yet, they are classified.

(120) Sword:11

> Sau   khi   th nh   t i,   nh   sư
> place^behind when succeed talent respected Buddhist^monk
> RN   GC   V   N<   [GC]   N
>
> tặng   cậu một   thanh gươm   qúi
> offer 3s   one/a sword sword be^noble/precious
> V   KIN NU   [MC]   N   SV

After graduation, the monk gave him a special sword...

(121) Sword:33

> Sau   đó   mãng x   từ   từ vắt   mǐnh qua
> after that boa   snake slowly <   pull^up self across
> RN   DM   AJ   N   SV   <   V   KIN   [V]
>
> bức tường
> wall wall
> MC   N

After that, the python slowly pulled itself across the wall...

The second characteristic of a classified NP in Vietnamese narrative is associated with the first characteristic. The first requirement for using a classifier is that the information must be important in the speaker's estimation. The second prerequisite tends to correlate with the first; the significant information presented as a classified NP must be new information or discontinuous reference. Based on the statistics from 4.8, this criterion appears to be fairly obligatory; the majority of discontinuous mentions in the data are classified NPs.

As properties of discourse, neither of the two major characteristics of classified NPs is evident in smaller syntactic environments such as individual sentences or clauses. Consequently, measurement and analysis of the discourse features associated with classifiers proves to be an apt method for identifying their function in Vietnamese narrative.

5.2. Modifying classifiers, general categoricals, and kin classifiers. Although subtypes of classifiers can be posited by dividing classifiers along syntactic or semantic lines, any functional differences between them must be understood in terms of their use in discourse. Based on the syntactic environments in which the words may appear, Thompson (1965) posits two major types of classifiers in Vietnamese: general categoricals (GC) which may be used as pronouns, while modifying classifiers (MC) may not. In terms of semantics, both categories refer to general classes of things, identifying single units, but MCs are more specific and definite in their categorizing function than GCs (Thompson 1965:193–97). In this study, the distribution of the two categories in discourse seemed at first to conform fairly consistently to Thompson's syntactic description. MCs are indeed used more strictly as descriptive complements than as pronouns; however, the two types are not really separate categories. The distribution patterns of MCs and GCs reveal a potential subtype of classifiers when the distribution of kin classifiers is also considered. The statistics distinguish kin classifiers as a potential subtype of classifier in that almost half of the GCs used as pronouns are actually kin classifiers. Rather than confirming the MC versus GC distinction, these findings support my analysis that kin classifiers are a middle category that exhibits syntactic, semantic, and discourse characteristics of both kin terms and classifiers. Like kin terms, kin classifiers are used to refer to individuals in terms of human relationship (e.g., the speaker's age in relation to the referent), and like classifiers, kin classifiers categorize referents with regard to a particular characteristic of that referent (e.g., male between the ages of eighteen and thirty). Given that their semantic domains overlap with the semantic domains of kin terms and classifiers, it is not surprising that the distribution of kin classifiers also reflects an overlap in the discourse functions of the two categories. Like kin terms, kin classifiers are often used pronominally (for direct address or third person reference), and like classifiers, kin classifiers are used with nouns, highlighting referential salience. The status of kin classifiers as a subtype of classifier is not apparent until the use of kin classifiers is examined in discourse, and conversely, the distinction between MCs and GCs is apparent until they are examined in discourse.

5.3. The advantages of discourse-based analysis. Discourse-based analysis allows the analyst to investigate a particular linguistic constituent or phenomenon in a context that has enough linguistic information to reveal the natural patterns of its use. The closer analysts can observe the natural use of a language, the more potential they have for capturing the systematic features in that language. Because language is always in process, the analyses which are the most authentic to the provisional nature of language best account for this flux. For example, one can explain some exceptions to linguistic patterns by considering the effects of grammaticalization. This approach suggests that a given part of speech has a source and a destination. Noun classifiers, for instance, have been cited as the diachronic source from which all class and gender features of pronouns emerge (Givón 1984a:384). Speakers begin to use classifiers with nouns to denote particular semantic categories, and over time, they begin to use them as pronouns. The use of some classifiers as pronouns can eventually give rise to definite articles. Although the hypotheses for the present research on classifiers in Vietnamese did not focus on classifiers with regard to their diachronic progression, the findings show that just over one-third of classifier use was pronominal. Moreover, among classifiers which were used five or more times in the data, 42% of the use was pronominal, and among classifiers which were used ten or more times, 46% of the use was pronominal. These results suggest that through higher frequency of use, a few classifiers in Vietnamese may be moving along the diachronic path from classifier to definite article. Similarly, the path of use of other grammatical features can be isolated and documented through discourse analysis. The discourse environment is large enough to capture a relatively wide scope of variation in use, yet small enough to allow practical analysis.

5.4–5.6 Implications of the study

5.4. Grammaticalization of classifiers. Diachronically, classifiers tend to evolve into pronouns or deictic pronouns, then definite articles. The more similar to a definite article a classifier becomes in terms of synchronic pattern, the less prototypically classifier it is. In terms of syntactic constructions and semantic function, the prototypical Vietnamese classifier appears next to a noun and categorizes some characteristic of that noun. While this research dispels the belief that

Conclusion 105

number + classifier + noun is the prototypical syntactic construction in Vietnamese, by the fact that merely 5% of the NPs in the data conform to this pattern, it confirms that classifier + noun is the prototypical construction. Sixty-six percent of the classified NPs in the data have this pattern. Some classifiers, such as the human classifiers *vi n* 'official' or *quan* 'mandarin', conform to the prototypical syntactic pattern with a higher frequency than other classifiers. Classifiers may deviate from this prototype over time, and, for example, may be used as pronouns with increasing frequency. This pattern is said to have taken place in Jacaltec (Mayan), where some classifiers are used as definite pronouns or definite articles; see example (122) (Givón 1984a).

(122) definite article   definite pronoun

    xul *naj* *Pel*   *xul* *naj*
    came person Peter   came person
    V   CL   NAM   V   CL

    Peter came.   He came.

By comparing the frequencies with which individual classifiers appear in prototypical versus nonprototypical constructions, one can gauge whether or not they are moving away from the classifier category on the classifier-to-definite article diachronic continuum. Several classifiers in the data for this study are possible candidates for having done this. While they are still used as other classifiers are used, words such as *người* 'person' and *con* 'offspring' are also often used as generic nouns. In that generic nouns are more definite than indefinite nouns are, the use of classifiers as generic nouns in Vietnamese may be associated with movement away from use as a strict classifier towards use as a definite pronoun, see examples (123)–(124).

(123) Mission:1, generic singular

      muốn *tìm* **người** *can*   *đảm*   *v*   *khôn* *ngoan*
      want   seek person courageous courage and wise be^a^schemer
      V   V   GC   AJ   N   CJ   AJ   SV

      wanted to find [a] brave and clever **person**

(124) Sword:2, generic plural

Nó	chuy n	môn	tìm	*người* ...
3s^ARROG	specialize^in	field^of^study	seek	person
PRO	V	GC	V	GC

đề̂	ăn	thịt
in^order^to	eat	flesh
CJ	V	N

It specialized in searching out **people**...in order to eat them.

5.5. Numeral or nominal? The term nominal is sometimes interchanged with numeral in reference to types of classifier languages, although the issue of whether or not they refer to separate linguistic systems remains to be settled. Citing several languages in which the syntactic use of classifiers rendered uncertain their status as either a numeral or a nominal classifier language, Greenberg (1977:279) cautions his readers:

> If all this [syntactic variation-KD] creates difficulties in establishing precise criteria based on syntactic function in numeral phrases, even graver problems arise in regard to classification as a definitional criterion...It is clear that many of the items that are listed as classifiers in grammars of numeral classifier languages cannot, in any reasonable view, be said to classify.

Hence, Greenberg recognizes the level of ambiguity involved in attempting to identify types of classifier systems on the basis of isolated syntactic or semantic properties. Congruent with this perspective, rather than being based solely on syntactic and semantic criteria, the present study is founded on the analysis of discourse features. The study shows that classifiers in Vietnamese function as a unified system of categorization, which brings into question the idea that the numeral and nominal classifier distinctions form two separate systems.

Classifiers in Vietnamese fit the description for both numeral and nominal types of classification systems. Numeral classifier languages are said to use classifiers in conjunction with quantification (e.g., 'three CL-animal buffaloes'), and nominal classifier languages are said to use classifiers independently of quantification (e.g., 'CL-revered king of Vietnam'). While classifiers in Vietnamese are used in both of these ways, in view of the findings of the present study, their use probably constitutes a single system. The findings for this study show that in discourse, classifiers function in the same way whether they appear with or without numbers. The majority of classifiers (76%) in the data appeared without numbers, and the majority of numbers (78%) appeared with classifiers. The high percentage of classifier use among numeral NPs can be explained in terms of the semantics of numbers as it relates to the discourse function of classifiers. Because cardinal numbers are not referential, they obligatorily occur with those constituents which are referential (noun, classifier NPs, or kin terms), and because cardinal numbers are specific, they are more likely than not to be used with salient referents. Inasmuch as a number points out a specific quantity associated with a referent, it is compatible with the function of a classifier to point out salient referents in discourse. Thus, the high frequency of classified numeral constructions is not contradictory with the even higher frequency of classified NPs without numbers in the same language. At least for Vietnamese, the use of classifiers implies a unified system of both numeral and nominal categorization.

5.6. Are all nouns classifiable? The results of this study with regard to the function of classifiers cast doubt on the claim that Vietnamese has nouns in its lexical inventory which do not take a classifier. According to Dyvik (1983:29–30), some nouns in Vietnamese are nonclassified, although nouns which are classified and those which are not classified do not constitute separate syntactic categories. If the argument were true that there were some nouns in Vietnamese which were not classifiable, it would imply the existence of some limitations on classifier use. In terms of the function of classifiers to mark referential salience, Vietnamese speakers would have to use a different linguistic device to mark nonclassifiable nouns as salient when those nouns were important referents. This scenario is entirely plausible; however, as a result of this research, I can now systematically explain why some nouns appear classified (they are referentially salient, and marked as such by a classifier) and why some nouns appear unclassified (they are not thematically prominent), and the argument is rendered irrelevant. The existence of unclassified nouns in Vietnamese can thus be understood as a consequence of speaker choice: speakers can choose not to code a referent as salient—they can choose not to classify a noun—or they can choose to code a referent as salient and classify the noun.

5.7–5.9 Directions for further research

5.7. Subtypes of classifiers. Despite the lack of evidence supporting the distinction between MC and GC, subsets of classifiers are distinguishable based on their functional distribution in discourse. For example, the classifier subset of kin classifiers are semantically similar to kin terms as well as to other human referent classifiers, so their distribution reflects the intersection of the two word classes. Kin classifiers may be used in direct address (as kin terms are), or they may be used in third person reference (as classifiers are). In addition, kin classifiers show a higher frequency of use as pronouns than other classifiers. Another classifier, *của* 'possession', may comprise a subtype in and of itself, given its uniqueness in meaning and distribution compared to other classifiers. Because of its definition, *của* must be used with animate referents, and it must not be used pronominally.

An additional question that should be answered with regard to classifiers that are used in time expressions is whether or not their function differs from that of other classifiers, given that their distribution clearly differs. For example, an informal count of time expressions in the data for this study reveals that 58% of time expressions contain at least one classifier, while only 33% of all the other NPs in the data (which were formally counted) contain at least one classifier. It is also immediately significant that almost 50% of classified time expressions occur clause initially, while only 21% of other classified NPs occur in this position. Hence, the clause internal distribution of other classified NPs does not reveal any clues about their discourse function. However, from these figures we can infer that the function of classifiers used in time expressions differs in a potentially important way from the function of other classifiers.

5.8. Classifiers and thematic continuity. In this study, I have illustrated that classifiers signal referent discontinuity, a function that is readily identifiable with topic or participant continuity. In relation to thematic continuity, participant continuity and action continuity can be thought of as subsets. The three types of discourse continuity may be understood as an inclusion set, whereby theme implies action implies participants. This implicational hierarchy of thematic continuity is shown in (125).

(125) THEME>ACTION>TOPICS / PARTICIPANTS

Conclusion

Each type of continuity is grammatically coded. For example, action continuity is associated with temporal adjacency and sequentiality within a thematic paragraph, and is typically marked in the tense, aspect, modality system (T.A.M. system) (Givón 1983). Because Vietnamese employs very little verbal marking, syntactic coding for action continuity is likely to be found elsewhere. Given that the classifiers in this study were found to code participant continuity, perhaps action continuity is coded by a type of classifier not considered in this study. Specifically, perhaps classifiers that do not refer to topics or participants, i.e., those in time expressions, signal discontinuity within or across thematic paragraphs.

Japanese speakers use classifiers for indicating peaks of the narrative or for rhetorical underlining. It may be that Vietnamese speakers use classifiers similarly. An analysis of classifier distribution with regard to these features, as well as to episode and thematic paragraph boundaries, should be pursued in future discourse studies of the Vietnamese classifier system.

5.9. Classifier use in other discourse genres. In this study I considered the use of classifiers in a single discourse genre, narrative. Consequently, the findings of this research are limited to that genre. Written discourse forms other than narrative text have different features, and classifiers may or may not function differently in them. Without question, spoken and written discourse also exhibit different properties. However, whether or not and to what extent the use of classifiers in conversational discourse differs from their use in written discourse is an issue for future study.

Appendix A
List of Classifiers in the Data and Additional Tables

List of Classifiers in the Data and Additional Tables   113

(126) Human classifiers in the data

Tag	Classifer	Gloss	Sword	Mission	Tinh	Mosquito	Total
GC	1. *con*	offspring	3	5	5	1	14
[KIN]	* *con*	[your child]	1	14	22	7	(44)
KCL	2. *ch ng*	young man	20	0	9	1	30
MC	3. *đứa*	lower class	0	5	0	0	5
[GC]	4. *kẻ*	person/individual	2	0	0	0	2
KCL	5. *n ng*	damsel	0	0	4	21	25
GC	6. *ng i*	[his] excellency	0	5	4	0	9
GC	7. *người*	person	11	9	7	9	36
[GC]	8. *nh*	king/monk	9	12	2	0	23
[GC]	9. *quan*	mandarin	1	1	0	0	2
[GC]	10. *vị*	[reverent]	0	9	0	1	10
[GC]	11. *vi n*	official	4	0	0	0	4
Total			50	46	31	33	160

The classifier *con* typically classifies a human referent, but may also be used to refer to an animal referent. A third homonym *con* is a kin term, listed here for interest. It is not included in any of the totals for classifiers.

Other possible classifiers are: (1) *lẽ* 'politeness' which appears in the data three times (Tinh S19, S33, and S40); in two instances, it occurs as part of a compound form and in the third instance is a possible classifier. (2) *ho ng* 'royal' which also appears three times in Tinh and may be a classifier instead of an adjective. The homonym/graphonym meaning 'fear' may also be related (appears once as the homonym in Sword).

(127) Nonhuman classifiers in the data

Tag		Classifer	Gloss	Sword	Mission	Tinh	Mosquito	Total
GC	1.	bao	scabbard/bag	1	4	0	0	5
[GC]	2.	bơ	bank (of a river)	1	0	0	0	1
MC	3.	bức	wall	1	0	0	0	1
MC	4.	c i	thing	1	0	1	0	2
[GC]	5.	căn	house	0	0	0	3	3
[GC]	6.	cây	tree	1	0	3	0	4
GC	7.	câu	sentence	0	1	0	0	1
MC	8.	chiếc	unit of	0	0	1	0	1
MC	9.	con	animal	10	9	0	1	20
GC	10.	của	possession	4	2	4	3	13
MC	11.	cuộc	existence	0	0	2	2	4
MC	12.	đ m	crowd	2	0	0	0	2
[MC]	13.	đồ	thing	0	0	2	0	2
GC	14.	đôi	pair	0	0	0	1	1
GC	15.	gi	valued/worth	0	0	1	0	1
[GC]	16.	giống	strain/breed	0	0	2	0	2
GC	17.	giọt	droplet	1	0	0	6	7
GC	18.	góc	corner	1	0	0	0	1
[GC]	19.	hạng	class/rank	0	0	1	2	3
GC	20.	l ng	village	1	10	0	2	13
GC	21.	lo i	species/type	0	0	2	0	2
GC	22.	lơi	spoken words	1	2	0	2	5
[GC]	23.	mảnh	fragment	3	0	0	0	3
[GC]	24.	môn	field of study	1	0	0	0	1
GC	25.	mùa	crop	0	0	1	0	1
[GC]	26.	mũi	point	1	0	0	0	1
[GC]	27.	ngh	trade	1	0	0	0	1
MC	28.	ngôi	temple	4	0	0	2	6
[MC]	29.	ngón	finger	0	0	0	3	3
GC	30.	nước	nation	0	3	1	0	4
[MC]	31.	quân	army	0	0	2	0	2
GC	32.	quả	fruit	0	0	1	0	1
[MC]	33.	sự	event	0	0	0	2	2
[MC]	34.	thanh	sword	2	0	0	0	2
GC	35.	thứ	order/rank	2	0	2	0	4
[GC]	36.	tiệc	banquet	1	0	0	0	1
GC	37.	tiếng	sound	2	0	1	0	3
GC	38.	trời	heaven/sky	0	1	2	3	6
[GC]	39.	vũng	puddle	1	0	0	0	1
Total nonhuman classifiers				43	32	29	32	136
Total human and nonhuman classifiers				93	78	60	65	296

List of Classifiers in the Data and Additional Tables 115

(128) Detail: Main and peripheral subjects in *A Broken Sword*

	Continuous						Discontinuous					
	CL	KIN	PRO	N	OTH	ZERO	CL	KIN	PRO	N	OTH	ZERO
snake	–	–	1	–	–	5	3	–	1	–	2	–
snake temple	1	–	–	–	–	–	–	–	1	–	–	–
y. man	8	3	–	–	–	15	9	1	–	–	–	1
sword	–	–	–	–	–	2	2	–	–	–	–	–
king	1	–	–	–	1	5	3	–	–	–	4	1
girl	–	2	–	–	–	1	1	2	–	–	–	–
patrol	–	–	2	–	–	4	3	–	–	–	–	–
periph	1	–	–	–	–	2	2	–	–	2	–	–
Total	11	5	3	0	1	34	23	3	2	2	6	2

(129) Detail: Main and peripheral objects in *A Broken Sword*

	Continuous						Discontinuous					
	CL	KIN	PRO	N	OTH	ZERO	CL	KIN	PRO	N	OTH	ZERO
snake	–	–	1	–	–	–	4	–	3	4	4	–
snake temple	–	–	–	1	–	–	3	–	–	3	–	1
y. man	–	–	–	–	–	–	3	2	–	2	–	1
sword	–	–	–	–	–	–	3	–	–	2	–	–
king	–	–	–	–	–	–	–	–	–	–	1	–
girl	–	1	–	–	–	–	–	2	–	–	–	–
patrol	–	–	–	–	–	–	1	1	1	–	–	–
periph	–	–	–	–	1	–	22	1	1	27	2	2
Total	0	1	1	1	1	0	36	6	5	38	7	4

(130) Detail: Classified and nominal peripheral objects in the discontinuous category in *A Broken Sword*

        Classified constructions   Noun phrases

1. * *người*   * *vùng núi nọ*
   'humans'   'another mountain region'
2. * *một mạng người con g i*   * *súc vật*
   'life (of a) young woman'   'livestock'
3. * *một ngôi chùa*   * *th t*
   'a Buddhist temple'   'flesh'
4. * *c c môn võ thật*   * *c ch*
   'various martial arts'   'way'
5. * *cả nghế múa gươm*   *vùng*
   'all (kinds of) fencing'   'region' (ref. to the people there)
6. * *l ng qu*   *t nh*
   'native village'   'disposition'
7. * *tiếng khóc*   * *ai*
   'sound (of) crying'   'anyone'
8. * *chuy n con mãng x*   * *công chúa*
   'story (of the) python'   'princess'
9. *một mạng người con g i*   * *núi cao*
   'life (of a) young woman'   '(a) high mountain'
10. * *bao*   * *th nh t i*
    'scabbard'   'graduation'
11. * *tiếng cây cối g y răng rắc*   * *phép*
    'sound (of) twigs snapping'   'permission'
12. * *bức tường*   *núi*
    'wall'   'mountain'
13. * *nh t thứ hai*   * *đường*
    '(a) second stab'   'road'
14. * *nh t thứ ba*   * *nước mắt*
    '(a) third stab'   'tears'
15. * *bờ suối*   *vùng*
    'banks (of a) stream'   'region'
16. * *vũng m u*   * *thân*
    'puddle (of) blood'   'fate'
17. *lời hứa của nh vua*   * *một ph t*
    'promise of the king'   'a blow'

18.	* d m cưới 'wedding procession'	* mấy vòng 'some circles'
19.	* một giọt m u 'one drop (of) blood'	* rừng 'forest'
20.	ti c cưới 'wedding banquet'	* suối 'stream'
21.	* ghế ch ng rể 'seat (of the) bridegroom'	* cung 'palace'
22.	d m cưới 'wedding procession'	thưởng 'reward'
23.	—	công chúa 'princess'
24.	—	* đền vua 'temple (of the) king'
25.	—	* vệ sĩ 'guard'
26.	—	* tù 'prison'
27.	—	công chúa 'princess'

In the above table, asterisked items are initial mentions: 82% (18 items) of CL are initial mentions, and 74% (20 items) of NPs are initial mentions.

Appendix B
Four Vietnamese Narrative Texts

Key to the interlinearized texts

ref	matrix clause number
tx	original text, in Vietnamese orthography
mg	morphemic gloss
gu	grammatical unit
ft	free translation

A Broken Sword
As told by Trần Văn Diến and Trần Cảnh Xuân (1993)

A Broken Sword is set in a legendary mountain kingdom of feudal era Vietnam. The conflict involves a python that has been terrorizing the kingdom by devouring people and livestock. The king has struck a deal with the python, agreeing that he will have one young maiden sacrificed to the python annually in exchange for peace in the kingdom. The king also offers a reward and the hand of the princess in marriage to the man who can kill the python. The hero is a young man who has been trained in sword fighting and martial arts by a Buddhist monk and is on his way back to his home village when he encounters the python's temple. He frees the python's current victim, slays the python, then goes to a forest near the python's temple to rest. A patrolman comes upon the dead python the next day and decides to take the python's head to the king and claim the reward for himself. They are in the midst of a wedding celebration when the young hero arrives at the king's palace to reclaim the fragment of his sword that remains lodged in the python's head. When the sword piece is extracted from the python's head and fits perfectly with the rest of the young man's sword, the patrolman is thrown into prison and the young man marries the princess.

ref   sword:1

tx   *Ng y xưa   tr n   vùng   núi   nọ   có*
mg   day past/former on/upon region mountain (an)other exist
gu   GC   AJ   RN   N   N   DM   V

tx   *một   con   mãng x .*
mg   one/a animal boa   snake
gu   NU   MC   N   N

ft   Once upon a time in another mountain region, there was a python.

ref   sword:2

tx   *Nó   chuy n   môn   tìm   người v*
mg   3s^ARROG specialize^in field^of^study seek person and
gu   PRO   V   [GC]   V   GC   CJ

tx	súc	vật	để		n	thịt.
mg	keep/raise	creature	in^order^to		eat	flesh
gu	V	N	CJ		V	N

ft   It specialized in searching out people and livestock in order to eat [them].

ref sword:3

tx	Dân	chúng	nghĩ	ra	đủ		c ch	để
mg	citizen	people	think	go^out	be^sufficient		way	in^order^to
gu	N	[QNF]	V	[V]	[SV]		N	CJ

tx	diệt	trừ	nó
mg	exterminate	remove	3s^ARROG
gu	V	V	PRO

ft   The citizens [tried to] figure out a way to destroy it

ref sword:4

tx	m	v n	không	kết	quả.
mg	but	still	not	conclude	result
gu	PRT	AUX	NG	V	N

ft   but still no resolution.

ref sword:5

tx	Con	qu i	vật	mỗi	ng y	một	trở	n n
mg	animal	be^odd	creature	every	day	one/a	become	<
gu	MC	[SV]	N	PL	GC	NU	V	<

tx	hung		dữ,	gây	kinh		ho ng	cho
mg	be^fierce^looking	<		bring	be^terrified		fear	for/until
gu	[SV]	<		V	[SV]		N	CJ

tx	cả		vùng.						
mg	all/the^whole		region						
gu	PRT		N						

ft Every day the monster became [more] fearsome, bringing terror to the whole region.

ref sword:6

tx	Vua	thấy	vậy	phải	sai	dựng	một	ngôi	đền
mg	King	perceive	so	must	command	build	one/a	temple	Temple
gu	N	V	DM	MD	V	V	NU	[MC]	N

tx	cho	nó	ở						
mg	for/until	3s^ARROG	live						
gu	CJ	PRO	V						

ft The king, perceiving this, had to order [them] to build a temple for it to live [in]

ref sword:7

tx	v	hứa	h ng	n m	dâng		nó	một
mg	and	promise	row/ranks	year	offer^respectfully		3s^ARROG	one/a
gu	CJ	V	[N]	GC	V		PRO	NU

tx	mạng	người	con	g i	để		nó	thuần
mg	life	person	offspring	girl	in^order^to		3s^ARROG	be^tamed
gu	N	GC	GC	N	CJ		PRO	[SV]

tx	t nh	lại.						
mg	disposition	again						
gu	N	[AV]						

ft and promised to offer it the life of a young girl every year in order for it to be tame again.

ref sword:8

tx	Nh	vua	cũng	hứa	ai	giết	chết	con	măng
mg	respected	King	likewise	promise	anyone	kill	die	animal	boa
gu	[GC]	N	PRT	V	IDN	V	V	MC	N

Four Vietnamese Narrative Texts 123

tx	x	sẽ	được		cưới	công	chúa.
mg	snake	shall	finish^successfully		marry	princess	<
gu	N	[MD]	ASP		V	N	<

ft   The king also promised [that] whoever killed the python would marry the princess.

ref   sword:9

tx	Thời	bấy	giờ,	có	ch ng		thanh	ni n	được
mg	then/time	then	time	exist	young^man		youth	<	[PASSIVE]
gu	N	DM	GC	V	KCL		N>	<	ASP

tx	một	nh	sư		nuôi	dưỡng	ở
mg	one/a	respected	Buddhist^priest		rear	support	be^located^in/at
gu	NU	[GC]	N		V	V	[SV]

tx	một	ngôi	chùa	tr n	núi		cao.
mg	one/a	temple	Temple	on/upon	mountain		be^high
gu	NU	[MC]	N	RN	N		[SV]

ft   At that time, in a pagoda on a high mountain there was a young man [who had been] raised by a Buddhist monk.

ref   sword:10

tx	H ng	ng y	nh	sư		dạy	cậu	c c
mg	row/ranks	day	respectcd	Buddhist^priest		teach	3s	various
gu	[N]	GC	[GC]	N		V	KIN	PL

tx	môn	võ	thuật	v	cả		nghề
mg	field^of^study	fighting	art/method	and	all/the^whole		trade
gu	[GC]	N	N	CJ	PRT		[GC]

tx	múa		gươm.
mg	ceremonial^dancing		sword
gu	N		N

ft   Daily, the Buddhist monk taught him various martial arts and all [kinds of] fencing.

ref   sword:11

tx   Sau   khi   th nh   t i,   nh
mg   place^behind when succeed talent/genius respected
gu   RN   GC   V   N<   [GC]

tx   sư   tặng   cậu một   thanh   gươm
mg   Buddhist^priest offer 3s   one/a stick/sword   sword
gu   N   V   KIN NU   [MC]   N

tx   qúi
mg   be^noble/precious
gu   [SV]

ft   After graduation, the Buddhist monk offered him a fine sword

ref   sword:12

tx   v   cho   phép   xuống   núi.
mg   and   give permission go^down   mountain
gu   CJ   V   N   V   N

ft   and gave [him] permission to descend the mountain.

ref   sword:13

tx   Tr n   đường   về   l ng   qu ,   ch ng   thanh
mg   on/upon   road   return village countryside young^man   youth
gu   RN   N   [V]   GC   N   KCL   N>

tx   ni n gặp   một   ngôi   đền,
mg   <   encounter   one/a temple Temple
gu   <   V   NU   [MC]   N

ft   On the way back to [his] native village, the young man came upon a temple

Four Vietnamese Narrative Texts

ref sword:14

tx	bèn	ghé	v o	nghỉ	chân.
mg	immediately	stop^off^at	enter	rest	foot/leg
gu	AV	V	[V]	V	N

ft [and] immediately stopped in to rest [his] legs.

ref sword:15

tx	Đó	l	đền	của	mãng	x
mg	that	be	Temple	possession	boa	snake
gu	DM	CP	N	GC	N	N

ft That was the python's temple

ref sword:16

tx	m	cậu	không	hay.
mg	but	3s	not	know
gu	PRT	KIN	NG	V

ft but he didn't know [it].

ref sword:17

tx	Vừa		tới	cổng	đền,	cậu	nghe	tiếng	khóc
mg	having^just^done		arrive	gate	Temple	3s	hear	sound	cry
gu	ASP		V	N	N	KIN	V	GC	V

tx	b n	trong.
mg	side	within
gu	[N]	[PRE]

ft Having just arrived at the temple gate, he heard the sound of crying inside.

ref   sword:18

tx	Bước	v o	đền,	cậu	thấy	một	cô	g i
mg	walk	enter	Temple	3s	perceive	one/a	young^woman	girl
gu	V	[V]	N	KIN	V	NU	KIN	N

tx	xinh	đ p,	tuổi	độ	18
mg	be^cute	be^beautiful	year^of^age	measure/time^period	18
gu	[SV]	[SV]	GC	[GC]	NU

tx	bị	trói	nằm	ở	góc	đền.
mg	[NEG^PASS]	tie	be^lying^down	be^located^in/at	corner	Temple
gu	ASP	V	[SV]	[SV]	GC	N

ft   Walking into the temple, he saw a pretty young woman about 18 years old, lying bound in the corner of the temple.

ref   sword:19

tx	Cậu	lập	tức	đến	cởi	trói	cho
mg	3s	establish	presently	come^to	unfasten	tie	for/until
gu	KIN	V	[GC]	[V]	V	V	CJ

tx	cô	g i
mg	young^woman	girl
gu	KIN	N

ft   He immediately came [and] untied the young woman

ref   sword:20

tx	v	hỏi,	'Tại	sao	cô	lại
mg	and	ask	why	how?	young^woman	act^contrary^to^expected
gu	CJ	V	INT	DM	KIN	V

tx	bị	trói	nằm	đây?'
mg	[NEG^PASS]	tie	be^lying^down	be^here
gu	ASP	V	[SV]	DM

ft   and asked, "Why are [you] lying here all tied up?"

ref	sword:21

tx	*Người*	*con*	*g i*	*lau*	*nước*	*mắt,*
mg	person	offspring	girl	wipe	liquid	eye
gu	GC	GC	N	V	N	N

ft	The girl wiped [her] tears.

ref	sword:22

tx	*'Ch ng*	*ở*	*đâu*	*tới?*	*Ch ng*	*không*
mg	young^man	be^located^in/at	where?	arrive	young^man	not
gu	KCL	[SV]	DM	V	KCL	NG

tx	*biết*	*đây*	*l*	*đền*	*mãng*	*x*	*sao?'*
mg	know	this	be	Temple	boa	snake	how
gu	V	DM	CP	N	N	N	DM

ft	"Where did [you] come from? Don't [you] know this is the python's temple?"

ref	sword:23

tx	*Cô*	*g i*	*tiếp*	*tục*	*kể*	*chuyện*	*con*	*mãng*
mg	young^woman	girl	continue	continue	tell	story	animal	boa
gu	KIN	N	V		ASP	V	N	MC	N

tx	*x .*
mg	snake
gu	N

ft	The young woman proceeded to tell the story of the python.

ref	sword:24

tx	*Cô*	*nói*	*mỗi*	*năm*	*dân*	*trong*
mg	young^woman	talk/tell	each	year	subject/citizen	within
gu	KIN	V	PL	GC	N	[PRE]

tx	vùng	phải	nộp	cho		mãng	x		
mg	region	must	submit	for/until		boa	snake		
gu	N	MD	V	CJ		N	N		

tx	một	mạng	người	con	g i	để	được	y n	thân.
mg	one/a	life	person	offspring	girl	for	[PASSIVE]	be^calm	fate
gu	NU	N	GC	GC	N	[PRE]	ASP	[SV]	N

ft The young woman said [that] each year a citizen in the region must submit the life of [their] daughter to the python in order for fate to be calmed.

ref	sword:25					
tx	Sau	cùng	cô	nức	nở,	'Thân
mg	place^behind	throughout	young^woman	sob	swell	fate
gu	RN	AJ	KIN	V	V	N

tx	em	có	chết	cũng	cam.	Chỉ	thương
mg	[here:1s]	be	die	likewise	be^resigned	only/just	love
gu	KIN	CP	V	PRT	[SV]	PRT	V

tx	cho	m	già	một	mình	không	ai	nuôi
mg	for^benefit^of	mother	old	one/a	self	not	anyone	rear
gu	PRT	KIN	AJ	NU	PRO	NG	IDN	V

tx	dưỡng.	Nhưng	thôi,	ch ng		hãy	mau	mau	ra
mg	support	but/yet	stop	young^man		be^sure^to	be^quick	<	exit
gu	V	CJ	V	KCL		[MD]	V	<	V

tx	khỏi	chốn	n y,	kẻo	mãng	x	về	thì	nguy
mg	escape	place	this	lest	boa	snake	return	then	perilous
gu	V	N	DM	CJ	N	N	[V]	PRT	AJ

tx	đến	t nh	mạng.'
mg	come^to	disposition	life
gu	[V]	N	N

ft Afterwards, the young woman sobbed, "[I] likewise am resigned [to the fact that] my fate is to die. Only, care for [my] elderly mother, [who is] alone without anyone to take care [of her]. But stop. [You] must leave this place at once lest the python returns, then [your] life will be in danger."

ref	sword:26							
tx	Ch ng	thanh ni n		không	do	dự,	'Tôi	muốn
mg	young^man	youth	<	not	be^hesitant	<	I	want
gu	KCL	N>	<	NG	[SV]	<	PRO	V

tx	nộp	mạng	thay	cô	để	cô
mg	submit	life	replace	young^woman	for	young^woman
gu	V	N	V	KIN	[PRE]	KIN

tx	được	về	săn	sóc	m	gìa.'
mg	be^able^to	return	look^after	<	mother	old
gu	ASP	[V]	V	<	KIN	AJ

ft The young man was not hesitant, "I want to submit [my] life for [yours], so [you] can go back to look after [your] elderly mother."

ref	sword:27						
tx	Cô	g i đ p,	'C m		ơn	ch ng,	nhưng
mg	young^woman	girl reply	appreciate	<		young^man	but
gu	KIN	N V	V	<		KCL	PRT

tx	em	không	muốn	ai	phải	chết	vì	em.
mg	[here:1s]	not	want	anyone	must	die	because^of	[here:1s]
gu	KIN	NG	V	IDN	MD	V	PRT	KIN

tx	Em	chỉ	xin	ch ng	có	dịp
mg	[here:1s]	only/just	request	young^man	exist	opportunity
gu	KIN	PRT	V	KCL	V	N

tx	ghé	thăm	v	săn	sóc	m	gìa	thay
mg	stop^off^at	visit	and	look^after	<	mother	old	replace
gu	V	V	CJ	V	<	KIN	AJ	V

tx	*em.'*
mg	[here:1s]
gu	KIN

ft The young woman replied, "Thank [you], but I don't want anyone to have to die because of me. I only ask [that if you] have the chance, stop by and look after [my] elderly mother in place of me."

ref sword:28

tx	*Người*	*thanh niên*	*cương*	*quyết,*	*'Không.*	*Cô*
mg	person	youth <	be^inflexible <		not	young^woman
gu	GC	N>	< V		< NG	KIN

tx	*hãy*	*đi*	*khỏi*	*nơi*	*nầy*	*ngay.*	*Để*
mg	be^sure^to	go	escape	place	this	immediately	[keep^on]
gu	[MD]	V	V	N	DM	AV	ASP

tx	*mặc*	*tôi*	*với*	*con*	*quái*	*vật.'*
mg	leave^alone	1p	against	animal	be^odd	creature
gu	V	PRO	PRE	MC	[SV]	N

ft The youth was insistent, "No. [You] should get out of this place immediately. Leave me alone [to go] against the monster."

ref sword:29

tx	*Rút*	*gươm*	*ra*	*khỏi*	*bao,*	*chàng*	*nói*
mg	pull^out	sword	come^out	escape	scabbard	young^man	talk/tell
gu	V	N	V	V	GC	KCL	V

tx	*tiếp,*	*'Đã*		*có*	*cái*	*nầy*	*nói*
mg	continue	[to^have^already]		possess	one^thing	this	talk/tell
gu	ASP	ASP		V	MC	DM	V

tx	*chuyện*	*với*	*nó.*	*Cô*		*đi*	*mau*
mg	conversation	against	3s^ARROG	young^woman		go	be^quick
gu	N	PRE	PRO	KIN		V	V

Four Vietnamese Narrative Texts 131

tx   đi.'
mg   [COMMAND]
gu   ASP

ft   Drawing a sword out of [its] scabbard, the young man went on talking: "[I] have this thing to say to it. [You] must go quickly!"

ref   sword:30

tx   Nói   xong,   người   thanh   ni n   d n   cô   g i
mg   talk/tell finish   person   youth   <   lead   young^woman   girl
gu   V   V   GC   N>   <   V   KIN   N

tx   ra   khỏi   đền
mg   come^out escape Temple
gu   V   V   N

ft   Having finished talking, the youth led the young woman out of the temple,

ref   sword:31

tx   rồi   trở   v o   cầm   kiếm   trong   tay   s n
mg   then   return enter take^hold^of foil   within   hand   have^ready
gu   [AV]   [V]   [V]   V   [N]   [PRE]   N   [SV]

tx   s ng   chờ   mãng   x   trở   về.
mg   <.   await   boa   snake   return   return
gu   <   V   N   N   [V]   [V]

ft   then came back in, taking the foil in hand, ready to await the python's return.

ref   sword:32

tx   V o   khoảng   nửa   đ m,   ch ng   bỗng   nghe   tiếng
mg   enter   interval   half   night   young^man   suddenly   hear   sound
gu   [V]   [GC]   N   GC   KCL   AV   V   GC

tx	cây	cối		g y	răng	rắc	ngo i	cổng	đền.
mg	tree	[shrubbery]		be^broken	tooth	crack	outside	gate	Temple
gu	[CAT]	N		[SV]	N	[V]	RN	N	N

ft   At about midnight, the young man suddenly heard the sound of twigs snapping outside the temple gate.

ref   sword:33

tx	Sau		đó	mãng	x	từ		từ vắt		mình	qua
mg	place^behind		that	boa	snake	be^slow		< pull^up		self	across
gu	RN		DM	N	N	[SV]		< V		PRO	[V]

tx	bức	tường	tiến	v o.
mg	wall	wall	advance	enter
gu	MC	N	[V]	[V]

ft   After that, the python slowly pulled itself across the wall, coming in.

ref   sword:34

tx	Ch ng	lanh	tay	chém	một	ph t	v o	đầu.
mg	young^man	be^agile	hand	chop	one/a	whack	enter	head
gu	KCL	[SV]	N	V	NU	N	[V]	N

ft   The deft young man struck one blow to the (python's) head.

ref   sword:35

tx	Con	qu i	vật	bị	thương	lao	tới
mg	animal	be^odd	creature	[NEG^PASS]	be^wounded	dizzy	advance
gu	MC	[SV]	N	ASP	[SV]	[AV]	[V]

tx	toan	nuốt	sống		kẻ
mg	attempt	swallow	complete/whole		person/individual
gu	V	V	AJ		[GC]

tx	*thù.*					
mg	be^enemy^with					
gu	[SV]					

ft   The monster, [which] had been wounded, dizzily advanced, attempting to swallow [his] enemy whole.

ref   sword:36

tx	*Nhưng*	*ch ng*		*thanh ni n*	*đã*	
mg	but/yet	young^man		youth <	[to^have^already]	
gu	CJ	KCL		N> <	ASP	

tx	*bồi*	*th m*	*nh t*	*thứ*	*hai.*
mg	follow^up^with	again	stab	order/rank	two
gu	V	[AV]	N	GC	NU

ft   But the young man had already followed up with a second stab.

ref   sword:37

tx	*Mãng x*	*đau*		*qu*	*k u*	*rống*
mg	boa snake	be^suffering		go^beyond	shout/complain	bellow
gu	N N	[SV]		[V]	V	V

tx	*l n*
mg	go^up
gu	[V]

ft   The deeply suffering python cried out,

ref   sword:38

tx	*rồi*	*quật*	*đuôi*	*tới*	*tấp*	*khiến*	*người*	*thanh ni n*	*ngã*
mg	then	whip	tail	advance <	cause	person	youth <	tumble
gu	[AV]	V	N	[V] <	V	GC	N> <	V

tx	lăn	đi	mấy	vòng.				
mg	roll	go	some	circle				
gu	V	V	IDN	N				

ft then whipped [its] tail, fast and thick, causing the youth to tumble in circles.

ref sword:39

tx	Sắp	bị	lọt	vɔ	miệng	con	quỉ
mg	be^about^to	[NEG^PASS]	fall^into	enter	mouth	animal	be^odd
gu	[SV]	ASP	V	[V]	N	MC	[SV]

tx	vật	thì	may		thay chɔ̀ng	đứng	dậy
mg	creature	then	be^lucky	<	young^man	stand^up	wake^up
gu	N	PRT	[SV]	<	KCL	V	V

tx	kịp
mg	in^time
gu	[AV]

ft [He was] about to fall into the monster's mouth when luckily the young man stood up in time

ref sword:40

tx	vɔ̀	đâm thɛ̂m	nhɔ́t	thứ	ba.	
mg	and	stab again	stab	order/rank	three	
gu	CJ	V [AV]	N	GC	NU	

ft and stabbed [it] again a third stab.

ref sword:41

tx	Nhưng	vì	đâm	mạnh	tay	quɔ́,	mũi	gươm
mg	but/yet	because^of	stab	be^strong	hand	excessive	point	sword
gu	CJ	PRT	V	[SV]	N	AJ	[GC]	N

tx	của	chàng	bị	gãy.
mg	possession	young^man	[NEG^PASS]	be^broken
gu	GC	KCL	ASP	[SV]

ft But because of the extremely strong-handed stabbing, the point of the young man's sword was broken.

ref sword:42

tx	Trong	lúc	hăng	say,	chàng	lăn	xả
mg	within	moment	be^ardent	be^drunk	young^man	roll	sacrifice
gu	[PRE]	[GC]	[SV]	[SV]	KCL	V	V

tx	tới	chặt	đứt	đầu	con	mãng xà.
mg	advance	chop	snap	head	animal	boa snake
gu	[V]	V	V	N	MC	N N

ft In a moment of fury, the young man rushed forward to chop off the python's head.

ref sword:43

tx	Giết	được	mãng xà	rồi,	chàng	khát
mg	kill	finish^successfully	boa snake	done	young^man	be^thirsty
gu	V	ASP	N N	[ASP]	KCL	[SV]

tx	nước	quá,
mg	liquid	go^beyond
gu	N	[V]

ft Having killed the python, the young man was excessively thirsty

ref sword:44

tx	bỏ	chạy	vô	rừng	tìm	suối	giải	khát.
mg	leave	run	enter	forest	seek	stream	>	be^thirsty
gu	V	V	[V]	N	V	N	V	[SV]

ft [so] ran off into the forest to find a stream to quench his thirst.

ref	sword:45							
tx	Uống	xong,	ch ng	mệt	mỏi	ngủ	lăn	b n
mg	drink	finish	young^man	be^exhausted	be^tired	sleep	roll	side
gu	V	V	KCL	[SV]	[SV]	V	V	[N]

tx	bờ	suối.
mg	bank	stream
gu	[GC]	N

ft Finished drinking, the exhausted young man [went to] sleep, rolling [over] beside the bank of the stream.

ref	sword:46						
tx	Ng y	hôm	sau,	một	vi n	l nh	tuần
mg	day	afternoon	place^behind	one/a	official	policeman	patrol
gu	GC	GC	RN	NU	[GC]	N	V

tx	đi	ngang	qua	ngôi	đền.
mg	go	be^horizontal	<	temple	Temple
gu	V	[SV]	<	[MC]	N

ft The next day a patrolman came across the temple.

ref	sword:47						
tx	Hắn	vô	cùng	ngạc	nhi n	thấy	mãng x
mg	3s	be^endless	the^end	choke	so	perceive	boa snake
gu	PRO	[SV]	N	V	CJ	V	N N

tx	nằm	chết	tr n	vũng	m u,	còn	cô	g i
mg	be^lying	die	on/upon	puddle	blood	remain	young^woman	girl
gu	[SV]	V	RN	[GC]	N	[V]	KIN	N

tx	thì	biến	đâu	mất.
mg	then	disappear	where?	be^lost
gu	PRT	V	DM	[SV]

ft He was extremely surprised to see the python lying dead in a puddle of blood, the young woman vanished.

ref   sword:48

tx   Nhớ   tới lời   hứa của   nh   vua,
mg   remember to   spoken^words vow possession   respected   King
gu   V   [V] GC   V   GC   [GC]   N

tx   hắn lập   tức   x ch   đầu   mãng x   về   cung
mg   3s   establish presently carry   head boa   snake return palace
gu   PRO V   [GC]   V   N   N   N   [V]   N

tx   xin   lãnh   thưởng.
mg   request receive reward
gu   V   V   N

ft   Remembering the king's promise, he immediately carried the python's head back to the palace to get the reward.

ref   sword:49

tx   Thấy   đầu   con   mãng x ,   nh   vua   mừng
mg   perceive head animal   boa   snake respected King be^pleased
gu   V   N   MC   N   N   [GC]   N   [SV]

tx   rỡ hỏi, 'Ai   đã   giết được   mãng
mg   < ask who?   [to^have^already] kill finish^successfully boa
gu   < V   IDN   ASP   V   ASP   N

tx   x ?'
mg   snake
gu   N

ft   Seeing the python's head, the exultant king asked, "Who has killed the python?"

ref   sword:50

tx   Vi n   l nh   tuần   hi n   ngang   trả
mg   official   policeman patrol be^haughty   <   give^back
gu   [GC]   N   V   [SV]   <   V

tx	lời,	'Tâu	bệ	hạ,	ch nh	
mg	spoken^words	[you^formal]	throne	beneath	precisely	
gu	GC	[PRO]	KIN	PRE	AV	

tx	kẻ	hạ	thần	n y.'
mg	person/individual	beneath	minister	this
gu	[GC]	PRE	N	DM

ft The haughty patrolman replied, "Your majesty, [it is] precisely this humble servant."

ref sword:51

tx	Nh	vua	liền	gả	công
mg	respected	King	act^immediately	give^for^marriage	princess
gu	[GC]	N	[V]	V	N

tx	chúa	cho	hắn	như	đã	hứa.
mg	<	for^benefit^of	3s	like	[to^have^already]	promise
gu	<	PRT	PRO	PRT	ASP	V

ft The king immediately gave the princess in marriage to him, as [he] had promised.

ref sword:52

tx	Đ m	cưới	được	tổ		chức	ngay	tại
mg	crowd	marry	[PASSIVE]	organize	<	immediately	be^at/in
gu	MC	V	ASP	V	<	AV	[SV]

tx	đền	vua.
mg	Temple	King
gu	N	N

ft The wedding procession was organized immediately in the king's temple.

ref sword:53

tx	Trong	lúc	quan	kh ch		tề	tựu
mg	within	moment	mandarin	person/visitor		regulate	come^near
gu	[PRE]	[GC]	[GC]	N[lit]		V	[V]

tx	đông đủ,	
mg	be^crowded be^sufficient	
gu	QNF [SV]	

ft Within a moment the guests assembled [until it was] sufficiently crowded

ref sword:54

tx	bỗng có người lạ mặt xin v o yết
mg	suddenly exist person strange face request enter call^on
gu	AV V GC AJ N V [V] V

tx	kiến vua.
mg	meet^with King
gu	V N

ft [and] suddenly there was a stranger requesting to meet with the king.

ref sword:55

tx	Người kh ch lạ n y ch nh l ch ng
mg	person person/visitor strange this precisely be young^man
gu	GC N[lit] AJ DM AV CP KCL

tx	thanh ni n đã giết con mãng x .
mg	youth < [to^have^already] kill animal boa snake
gu	N> < ASP V MC N N

ft This mysterious visitor was precisely the young man [who] had killed the python.

ref sword:56

tx	Vua hỏi, 'Nh người tới đây có
mg	King ask respected inferior(s) arrive be^here possess
gu	N V [GC] N V DM V

tx	chuyện	gì?'					
mg	conversation	what?					
gu	N	IDN					

ft The king asked, "What conversation did my subject come here to have?"

ref sword:57

tx	Ch ng	thanh ni n	thưa,		'Tâu	bệ	
mg	young^man	youth	<	reply^politely	[you^FORMAL]	throne	
gu	KCL	N>	<	PRT	[PRO]	KIN	

tx	hạ,	con	đến	xin	lại	mảnh	gươm
mg	beneath	[your^child]	come^to	request	again	fragment	sword
gu	PRE	KIN	[V]	V	[AV]	[GC]	N

tx	g y	còn	dắt	trong	đầu	mãng	x .'
mg	be^broken	remain	carry	within	head	boa	snake
gu	[SV]	[V]	V	[PRE]	N	N	N

ft The young man replied politely, "Your majesty, I came to request the broken sword fragment left lodged in the python's head."

ref sword:58

tx	Nh	vua	hết	sức	ngạc	nhi n,	đưa	mắt
mg	respected	King	complete	strength	choke	so	give	eye
gu	[GC]	N	V	N	V	CJ	V	N

tx	nhìn	chú	rể.
mg	look^at	[various]	son/brother^in^law
gu	V	KIN	KIN

ft The king, extremely surprised, cast a glance at the bridegroom.

ref sword:59

tx	Lúc	đó,	mặt	vi n	l nh	tuần	t i	x m,
mg	moment	that	face	official	policeman	patrol	be^pale	be^grey
gu	[GC]	DM	N	[GC]	N	V	[SV]	[SV]

tx	cắt	không	còn	một	giọt	máu.
mg	cut^off	not	remain	one/a	droplet	blood
gu	V	NG	[V]	NU	GC	N

ft That moment, the patrolman's face was pale, [as if] cut off [so that] not one droplet of blood remained [in it].

ref sword:60

tx	Vua	liền		cho	hoãn	tiệc	cưới
mg	King	act^immediately	cause	postpone	banquet	marry
gu	N	[V]	V	V	[GC]	V

ft The king immediately caused the postponement of the wedding banquet,

ref sword:61

tx	rồi	sai	vệ	sĩ	bổ	đầu	mãng	x	tìm	mảnh
mg	then	command	guard	<	split	head	boa	snake	seek	fragment
gu	[AV]	V	V	<	V	N	N	N	V	[GC]

tx	gươm.
mg	sword
gu	N

ft then commanded the guard to split the python's head to search for the fragment of the sword.

ref sword:62

tx	Quả	thật,	mảnh	gươm	đã		được
mg	indeed	be^genuine	fragment	sword	[to^have^already]	[PASSIVE]
gu	[PRT]	[SV]	[GC]	N	ASP	ASP

tx	tìm	thấy.
mg	seek	perceive
gu	V	V

ft Indeed, [the] sword fragment had been found.

ref sword:63

tx	Đem	r p	v o	thanh	gươm	của		người
mg	take/bring	join	enter	stick/sword	sword	possession		person
gu	V	V	[V]	[CL]	N	GC		GC

tx	thanh ni n	thì		vừa	kh t.
mg	youth <	then		fit	be^well^joined
gu	N> <	PRT		V	[SV]

ft [When] brought together with the youth's sword, [it] was a perfect fit.

ref sword:64

tx	Lập	tức	vua	sai	bỏ	tù	vi n
mg	establish	presently	King	command	leave	prison	official
gu	V	[GC]	N	V	V	N	[GC]

tx	l nh	tuần.
mg	policeman	patrol
gu	N	V

ft Immediately the king commanded [them] to put the patrolman in prison.

ref sword:65

tx	Sau	đó	vua	dắt	người	thanh ni n	tới	ngồi	ghế
mg	place^behind	that	King	lead	person	youth <	to	sit	seat
gu	RN	DM	N	V	GC	N> <	[V]	V	N

tx	ch ng	rể		b n	cạnh	công	chúa
mg	young^man	son/brother^in^law		side	edge	princess	<
gu	KCL	KIN		[N]	GC	N	<

ft After that, the king led the youth to sit [in] the bridegroom's seat next to the princess,

Four Vietnamese Narrative Texts

ref	sword:66							
tx	rồi	truyền	cho	đám	cưới	lại	tiếp	tục
mg	then	order	for/until	crowd	marry	again	continue	continue
gu	[AV]	V	CJ	MC	V	[AV]	V	ASP

tx	như	cũ.
mg	like	<
gu	PRT	<

ft then ordered the wedding procession to continue again as before.

Mission Impossible
As told by Trần Văn Diến and L Tinh Thông (1992)

Mission Impossible is a tale set in feudal Vietnam, in which an elderly king sends his advisors throughout the countryside in search of a gifted young man to help him govern the country. One of the king's advisors encounters a young farm boy and his father, plowing a field with their buffalo. The advisor asks them a trick question, and instead of answering the question, the boy turns the question around on the advisor. The advisor, impressed with the response, reports the incident to the king. The king then orders the advisor to deliver three male buffaloes and three bags of rice to the boy's village with instructions for the villagers. They are to breed nine buffaloes by the next year, or the whole village will be punished. After no one in the village can resolve the problem, the farm boy suggests to the village elders that they slaughter two of the buffaloes and cook two bags of rice for the villagers to have a feast in honor of the king. The boy then takes the remaining buffalo and rice with him to the king's palace to address the king. He tells the king the sad story of how he longs for a baby brother, so prays every night that his widower father would give him a sibling. The king chides the boy for thinking a man can bear a child, to which the boy remarks that the same principle is true for buffaloes. The king rewards the boy for his cleverness by naming him trusted courtier.

ref   mission:1

tx	Ng y	xưa,		có	vị		vua	Việt-Nam	muốn	tìm
mg	day	past/former		exist	revered		King	Vietnam	want	seek
gu	GC	AJ		V	[GC]		N	NAM	V	V

tx	người	can		đảm	v	khôn	ngoan		để	giúp
mg	person	courageous		courage	and	wise	be^a^schemer		for	help
gu	GC	AJ		N	CJ	AJ	SV		[PRE]	V

tx	việc	trị	nước.
mg	concern	govern	nation
gu	N	V	GC

ft   Once upon a time, [there] was a Vietnamese king [who] wanted to find a courageous and wise person for an assistant [in] governing the nation.

Four Vietnamese Narrative Texts 145

ref mission:2

tx	Ng i	cử	c c	vị	cố-vấn	đi
mg	[his]excellency	appoint	various	revered	advisor	go
gu	GC	V	PL	[GC]	N	V

tx	khắp	nước	để	tìm	người	xứng	d ng.
mg	everywhere/all	nation	for	seek	person	worthy	<
gu	AJ	GC	[PRE]	V	GC	AJ	<

ft He apointed various advisors to go all over the country to find a suitable person.

ref mission:3

tx	Một	buổi	chiều,	một	vị	cố-vấn	nh
mg	one/a	time^period	afternoon	one/a	revered	advisor	respected
gu	NU	GC	[GC]	NU	[GC]	N	[GC]

tx	vua	đi	ngang	qua	c nh	đồng	thấy	một	người
mg	King	go	across	by/through	field	tree	perceive	one/a	person
gu	N	V	[V]	CJ	N	N	V	NU	GC

tx	đ n	ông	v	đứa	con
mg	[HONORIFIC]	male^relative	and	[lower^rank]	offspring
gu	KIN	KIN	CJ	MC	GC

tx	trai	đang	c y	ruộng	với	con	trâu,
mg	young^man	be^in^process^of	plough	field	with	animal	buffalo
gu	N	ASP	V	N	[V]	MC	N

tx	liền	đứng	lại	hỏi,	'Con
mg	act^immediately	stand^up	come[short^distance]	ask	animal
gu	[V]	V	V	V	MC

tx	trâu	c c	anh	c y	được
mg	buffalo	various	close^male^relative	plough	finish^successfully
gu	N	PL	KIN	V	ASP

tx	bao	nhi u	luống	một	ng y?
mg	ever	abundant	furrow	one/a	day
gu	DM	AJ	N	NU	GC

ft One afternoon, one of the king's counselors came by a field [and] saw a man and his son plowing the field with a buffalo, [and he] immediately stopped to ask: "How many furrows can your (plural) buffalo finish ploughing [in] one day?"

ref mission:4

tx	Người	nông	dân	ngạc	nhi n	trước	câu
mg	person	farming	subject/citizen	choke	so	before	sentence
gu	GC	N	N	V	CJ	AV	GC

tx	hỏi	kỳ	lạ	đó.
mg	ask	strange	strange	that
gu	V	AJ	AJ	DM

ft The farmer was surprised at that strange question.

ref mission:5

tx	Nhưng	đứa	con	trai	của
mg	but/yet	[lower^rank]	offspring	young^man	possession
gu	CJ	MC	GC	N	GC

tx	ông	không	phải	nghĩ	ngợi	lâu.
mg	male^relative	not	must	think	<	long^while
gu	KIN	NG	MD	V	<	N

ft But the son of the man did not have to ponder [it] long.

ref mission:6

tx	Nó	hỏi	lại	vị	cố-vấn	nh	vua,
mg	3s^ARROG	ask	in^return	revered	advisor	respected	King
gu	PRO	V	[AV]	[GC]	N	[GC]	N

tx	'Dạ	thưa	Ng i,	xin
mg	[courteous]	reply^politely	[his]excellency	request
gu	[FW]	PRT	GC	V

tx	Ngài		có	thể	cho	chừu		biết
mg	[his]excellency		possess	may	allow	[young^relative]		know
gu	GC		V	MD	V	KIN		V

tx	con	ngựa	của	Ngài		đi	được	
mg	animal	horse	possession	[his]excellency		go	finish^successfully	
gu	MC	N	GC	GC		V	ASP	

tx	mấy		bước	trong	một	ngày	không	ạ.'
mg	any^amount^of		step	within	one/a	day	not	sir/madam
gu	PRO		N	[PRE]	NU	GC	[QW]	[FW]

ft He asked in reply [to] the king's advisor, "Your excellency, could his excellency please let me know how many steps the horse of his excellency completes within a day?"

ref mission:7

tx	Vị	cố-vấn	nhà	vua	không	trả	lời
mg	revered	advisor	respected	King	not	give^back	spoken^words
gu	[GC]	N	[GC]	N	NG	V	GC

tx	được	và	thầm	nghĩ,	'Thằng	bé	này	tinh
mg	be^able^to	and	secret	think	kid	small	this	quick^witted
gu	ASP	CJ	AJ	V	KIN	AJ	DM	AJ

tx	khôn	thật.
mg	wise	actual/true
gu	AJ	AJ

ft The king's advisor could not reply and secretly thought, "This little kid [is] truly clever!"

ref mission:8

tx	Ông	liền		cỡi	ngựa	về	triều-đình
mg	gentleman	act^immediately		ride	horse	return	royal^court
gu	KIN	[V]		V	N	[V]	N

tx	tâu	lại	với	Vua	về	cậu bé	nh
mg	address	again	toward	King	about	3s small	dwelling
gu	V	[AV]	PRE	N	CJ	KIN AJ	N

tx	qu	đó.
mg	countryside	that
gu	N	DM

ft The gentleman immediately rode [his] horse back to the royal court [and] addressed the king again about that young country boy.

ref mission:9

tx	Nghe	truyện,	nh	vua	rất	mừng	v	muốn	thử
mg	hear	story	respected	King	very	be^pleased	and	want	try
gu	V	N	[GC]	N	AV	[SV]	CJ	V	V

tx	t i		cậu	bé	đó	lần	nữa.
mg	talent/genius	3s	small	that	time	another
gu	N		KIN	AJ	DM	GC	PRT

ft Hearing the story, the king was very pleased and wanted to test that young boy's talent another time.

ref mission:10

tx	Nh	vua	nói	với	vị	cố-vấn,	'Người
mg	respected	King	talk/tell	toward	revered	advisor	person
gu	[GC]	N	V	PRE	[GC]	N	GC

tx	hãy	đem	ba	con	trâu	đực	v	ba	bao
mg	be^sure^to	take/bring	three	animal	buffalo	male	and	three	bag
gu	[MD]	V	NU	MC	N	AJ	CJ	NU	GC

tx	gạo	tới	l ng	đứa		bé	đó.
mg	rice	to	village	[lower^rank]		small	there
gu	N	[V]	GC	MC		AJ	DM

ft The king said to the advisor, "You must take three male buffaloes and three bags of rice to that little boy's village."

ref   mission:11

tx   Hãy   bảo   dân   l ng   nuôi   ba   con
mg   be^sure^to   say   subject/citizen   village breed three animal
gu   [MD]   V   N   GC   V   NU   MC

tx   trâu   n y   cho   chúng   để   th m   ch n
mg   buffalo this for/until   [PLURAL^person]   give^birth^to   add   nine
gu   N   DM   CJ   PRO   V   [V]   NU

tx   con   nữa   v o   năm   tới.
mg   offspring   more   enter   year   arrive
gu   GC   AV   [V]   GC   V

ft   "Tell the villagers to breed these three buffaloes for them to give birth to nine more offspring by next year."

ref   mission:12

tx   Nếu   họ   không   l m   được,   ta   sẽ   truyền   phạt
mg   if   3p   not   do/make   be^able^to   1s^SUP   shall   order   punish
gu   CJ   PRO   NG   V   ASP   PRO   [MD]   V   V

tx   hết   cả   l ng.'
mg   complete   all/the^whole   village
gu   V   PRT   GC

ft   "If they aren't able to, I shall order [that] the entire village [be] punished."

ref   mission:13

tx   Nghe   lệnh   đó   dân   l ng   lo   sợ
mg   hear   decree   that   subject/citizen   village   worry   be^afraid
gu   V   N   DM   N   GC   V   SV

tx	qu	vì		họ	không	biết	phải l m	gì.
mg	excessive	because^of		3p	not	know	must do/make	what
gu	AJ	PRT		PRO	NG	V	MD V	IDN

ft Hearing that decree, the villagers were excessively anxious because they did not know what [they] had to do.

ref mission:14

tx	C c	vị	kỳ	lão	trong	l ng	hội họp
mg	various	revered	admin^division	old	within	village	meet gather
gu	PL	[GC]	N	AJ	[PRE]	GC	V V

tx	nhau	b n	kế	thi	h nh	lệnh	vua
mg	each^other	discuss	stratagem	execute	perform	decree	King
gu	PRT	V	N	V	V	N	N

tx	nhưng	cũng	không có	kết	quả.		
mg	but	all^the^same	not possess	conclude	result		
gu	PRT	PRT	NG V	V	N		

ft The elders in the village met together to discuss a strategem to carry out the king's decree, but all the same, [they] had no results.

ref mission:15

tx	Cả	l ng	họp	lại	m	không	ai	l m
mg	all/the^whole	village	gather	again	but	not	anyone	do/make
gu	PRT	GC	V	[AV]	PRT	NG	IDN	V

tx	gì	được.
mg	what	be^able^to
gu	IDN	ASP

ft The whole village gathered again, but no one could do anything.

ref mission:16

tx	Bấy	giờ	cậu	bé	con	người	nông	dân
mg	then	time	3s	small	offspring	person	farming	subject/citizen
gu	DM	GC	KIN	AJ	GC	GC	N	N

tx	liền		thưa,	'Ch u		thi
mg	act^immediately		reply^politely	[young^relative]		execute
gu	[V]		[V]	KIN		V

tx	h nh	được	lệnh	nh	vua.
mg	perform	be^able^to	decree	respected	King
gu	V	ASP	N	[GC]	N

ft   At that time the farmer's boy respectfully responded, "I can carry out the king's decree."

ref   mission:17

tx	Xin	giao	cho	ch u	một	con	trâu	v
mg	request	entrust	to	[young^relative]	one/a	animal	buffalo	and
gu	V	V	PRT	KIN	NU	MC	N	CJ

tx	một	bao	gạo.
mg	one/a	bag	rice
gu	NU	GC	N

ft   "Please give me one buffalo and one bag of rice."

ref   mission:18

tx	Hai	con	còn	lại	thì	đem	l m	thịt
mg	two	animal	remain	moreover	then	take/bring	do/make	meat
gu	NU	MC	[V]	PRT	PRT	V	V	N

tx	v	nấu	hai	bao	gạo	cho	cả	l ng	ăn
mg	and	boil	two	bag	rice	for/until	all/the^whole	village	eat
gu	CJ	V	NU	GC	N	CJ	PRT	GC	V

tx	nhậu.
mg	booze
gu	V

ft   "Then, in addition, take the remaining two [and] butcher [them] and boil the two bags of rice for the whole village to feast on."

ref	mission:19							
tx	Ăn	xong	chúng	ta	cùng	nhau	tạ	ơn
mg	eat	finish	[PLURAL^person]	1s^SUP	same	each^other	thank	favor
gu	V	V	PRO	PRO	AJ	PRT	V	N

tx	Đức	vua	vì	Ng i		thật	l	
mg	virtuous	King	because^of	[his]excellency		actual/true	be	
gu	AJ	N	PRT	GC		[AV]	CP	

tx	vị	vua	cao	cả	v	nhân	từ.'	
mg	revered	King	be^high	all/the^whole	and	benevolence	kind	
gu	[GC]	N	[SV]	PRT	CJ	N	AJ	

ft "We [will] eat [it] up together, thanking [our] virtuous king because his excellency is truly the greatest and [most] kind-hearted."

ref	mission:20							
tx	V i	ng y	sau	cậu	bé	đi	với	cha	đến
mg	a^few	day	place^behind	3s	small	go	with	father	come^to
gu	AJ	GC	RN	KIN	AJ	V	[V]	KIN	[V]

tx	xin	yết	kiến	vua.
mg	request	call^on	meet^with	King
gu	V	V	V	N

ft A few days later the boy accompanied [his] father to request an interview with the king.

ref	mission:21								
tx	Cậu	để		cha	đợi	b n	ngo i	v	một	mình
mg	3s	leave^behind	father	wait^for	side	outside	and	one/a	self
gu	KIN	V	KIN	V	[N]	RN	CJ	NU	PRO

Four Vietnamese Narrative Texts

```
tx   đi   v    o      cung    yết         kiến       Đức       vua.
mg   go   enter palace call^on meet^with   virtuous  King
gu   V    [V]  N      V                   AJ        N
```

ft   He left [his] father waiting outside and went by himself into the palace to meet with the king.

ref mission:22

```
tx   Cậu  quì    xuống    trước   mặt  vua   v    bắt    đầu       khóc.
mg   3s   kneel  go^down  before  face King  and  start  beginning cry
gu   KIN  V      V        AV      N    N     CJ   V      N         V
```

ft   He knelt down in front of the king and began to cry.

ref mission:23

```
tx   Nh       vua   mới           hỏi  cậu  tại      sao
mg   respected King [right^then]  ask  3s   due^to   how?
gu   [GC]     N     PRT           V    KIN  AV       DM

tx   lại                        khóc.
mg   act^contrary^to^expected   cry
gu   V                          V
```

ft   The king then asked him why he was crying.

ref mission:24

```
tx   Cậu  liền             thưa,          'Tâu           Bệ
mg   3s   act^immediately  reply^politely [you^FORMAL]   throne
gu   KIN  [V]              [V]            [PRO]          KIN

tx   hạ,       con           mồ      côi  m    từ           lúc
mg   beneath   [your^child]  orphan  <    mother since/from moment
gu   PRE       KIN           SV      <    KIN  CJ           [GC]
```

tx	còn nhỏ.
mg	still young
gu	AUX [SV]

ft	He immediately replied, "Your Majesty, I have been motherless since I was young."

ref	mission:25

tx	Bây	giờ	con		ở	với	cha	con.
mg	right^now	time	[your^child]		live	with	father	[your^child]
gu	DM	GC	KIN		V	[V]	KIN	KIN
ft	"Now I live with my father."							

ref	mission:26

tx	Con	mơ	ước	có	được	một
mg	[your^child]	dream/wish	wish	possess	be^able^to	one/a
gu	KIN	V	V	V	ASP	NU

tx	đứa	em	trai.
mg	[lower^rank]	younger^sibling	young^man
gu	MC	KIN	N

ft	"I wish I could have a younger brother."

ref	mission:27

tx	Con	cầu	trời	mỗi	đ m	để	cha
mg	[your^child]	pray^to	heaven	each	night	for	father
gu	KIN	V	GC	PL	GC	[PRE]	KIN

tx	con	sinh	cho		một	đứa
mg	[your^child]	give^birth^to	for^benefit^of		one/a	[lower^rank]
gu	KIN	V	PRT		NU	MC

tx	em	trai.
mg	younger^sibling	young^man
gu	KIN	N

ft	"I pray to heaven each night that my father would give birth to a younger brother for me."

ref   mission:28

tx   Nhưng   cha   con   không   t i   n o
mg   but/yet father   [your^child]   not   talented/gifted at^all
gu   CJ   KIN   KIN   NG   [SV]   DM

tx   l m   được.
mg   do/make   be^able^to
gu   V   ASP

ft   "But my father [is] not at all gifted to be able to do [this]."

ref   mission:29

tx   Ch nh   vì   vậy   con   buồn
mg   precisely   because^of   thus   [your^child]   sad/melancholy
gu   AV   PRT   DM   KIN   [SV]

tx   m   khóc.'
mg   as^a^result   cry
gu   CJ   V

ft   "This [is] precisely why I am sad and cry."

ref   mission:30

tx   Nh   vua   nghe   cậu bé   kể   chuyện   liền
mg   respected   King   hear   3s small   tell   story   act^immediately
gu   [GC]   N   V   KIN AJ   V   N   [V]

tx   cười   m   ph n   rằng,   'Sao   con   khờ
mg   laugh   as^a^result   command   saying how?   [your^child]   naive
gu   V   CJ   V   PRT   DM   KIN   [SV]

tx   qu   vậy.
mg   excessive   thus
gu   AJ   DM

ft   Upon hearing the boy tell the story the king laughed then said, "How [can] you [be] so naive as this?"

ref   mission:31

tx	Nếu	con		muốn	có	em		trai	
mg	if	[your^child]		want	possess	younger^sibling		young^man	
gu	CJ	KIN		V	V	KIN		N	

tx	thì	hãy		xin	cha	con	cưới	vợ	kh c
mg	then	be^sure^to		request	father	[your^child]	marry	wife	other
gu	PRT	[MD]		V	KIN	KIN	V	N	AJ

tx	nữa	đi.
mg	again	[COMMAND]
gu	PRT	ASP

ft "If you want to have a younger brother, then [you] must ask your father to marry again."

ref   mission:32

tx	Cha	con	l	đ n	ông	l m	sao
mg	father	[your^child]	be	[HONORIFIC]	male^relative	so	how?
gu	KIN	KIN	CP	KIN	KIN	[V]	DM

tx	sinh	được?'
mg	give^birth^to	be^able^to
gu	V	ASP

ft "Your father is a man, so how can he give birth?"

ref   mission:33

tx	Cậu bé	trả	lời	ngay,	'Dạ,
mg	3s small	give^back	spoken^words	immediately	[courteous]
gu	KIN AJ	V	GC	AV	[FW]

tx	Đức	vua	có	lý.
mg	virtuous	King	possess	reason/grounds
gu	AJ	N	V	N

ft The boy immediately replied, "Your majesty makes sense."

```
ref    mission:34

tx     Nhưng   tuần   vừa       qua         ch nh       Đức       vua
mg     but/yet week   just^now  by/through  precisely   virtuous  King
gu     CJ      GC     AV        CJ          AV          AJ        N

tx     đã                 cho    l ng     con           ba     con     trâu
mg     [to^have^already]  give   village  [your^child]  three  animal  buffalo
gu     ASP                V      GC       KIN           NU     MC      N

tx     đực   v    ra       lệnh    năm   tới     phải  sản      xuất     th m
mg     male  and  go^out   decree  year  arrive  must  produce  go^out   add
gu     AJ    CJ   [V]      N       GC    V       MD    V        [V]      [V]

tx     ch n  trâu     con.
mg     nine  buffalo  offspring
gu     NU    N        GC

ft     "But last week his majesty the king himself gave my village
       three male buffaloes and gave the order to produce nine more
       offspring next year."

ref    mission:35
tx     Cả                l ng     rất   lo      lắng    vì          không
mg     all/the^whole     village  very  worry   settle  because^of  not
gu     PRT               GC       AV    V       V       PRT         NG

tx     biết  phải  l m       sao.'
mg     know  must  do/make   how?
gu     V     MD    V         DM

ft     "The whole village was very worried because [we] did not know
       how to do [it]."

ref    mission:36

tx     Nh         vua   lại    cười   rồi    nói,        'Ta     chỉ
mg     respected  King  again  laugh  then   talk/tell   1s^SUP  only/just
gu     [GC]       N     [AV]   V      [AV]   V           PRO     PRT
```

tx	muốn thử	c c	người	m	thôi.	
mg	want try	various	person	but	only/just	
gu	V V	PL	GC	PRT	PRT	

ft The king laughed again, then said, "I only wanted to test you all, that's all."

ref mission:37

tx	Ta	đã	cho	c c	người	ba	bao gạo.
mg	1s^SUP	[to^have^already]	give	various	person	three	bag rice
gu	PRO	ASP	V	PL	GC	NU	GC N

ft "I gave you all three bags of rice."

ref mission:38

tx	Vậy	tại	sao	không	l m	thịt	mấy con	trâu
mg	thus	due^to	how?	not	do/make	meat	some animal	buffalo
gu	DM	AV	DM	NG	V	N	IDN MC	N

tx	đó	ăn nhậu	một	bữa	cho	ngon?'	
mg	that	eat booze	one/a	meal	for/until	tasty	
gu	DM	V V	NU	N	CJ	AJ	

ft "So, why don't you slaughter some of those buffaloes for a big, delicious feast?"

ref mission:39

tx	Cậu bé	thưa,	'Dạ,	Đức	vua	thật
mg	3s small	reply^politely	[courteous]	virtuous	King	actual/true
gu	KIN AJ	[V]	[FW]	AJ	N	AJ

tx	l	một vị	vua	cao	cả.
mg	be	one/a revered	King	be^high	all/the^whole
gu	CP	NU [GC]	N	[SV]	PRT

ft The boy replied respectfully, "Your majesty is truly a great king."

ref	mission:40						
tx	Cả	l ng	con	đã		ăn	nhậu
mg	all/theˆwhole	village	[yourˆchild]	[toˆhaveˆalready]		eat	booze
gu	PRT	GC	KIN	ASP		V	V

tx	tối	qua	rồi.'
mg	night	by/through	already
gu	GC	CJ	[AV]

ft "Our whole village already feasted last night."

ref	mission:41							
tx	Nh	vua	thấy	rõ	cậu	bé	đúng	l người
mg	respected	King	perceive	clear	3s	small	sound/true	be person
gu	[GC]	N	V	AJ	KIN	AJ	AJ	CP GC

tx	mình	đang		tìm.
mg	self	beˆinˆprocessˆof		seek
gu	PRO	ASP		V

ft The king clearly saw the boy truly was the person he was looking for.

ref	mission:42							
tx	Chắc	chắn	cậu	sẽ	trở	th nh	vĩ-nhân	v
mg	beˆcertain	barrier	3s	shall	become	turnˆinto	greatˆman	and
gu	SV	N	KIN	[MD]	V	V	N	CJ

tx	giúp	mình	trị	nước.
mg	help	self	govern	nation
gu	V	PRO	V	GC

ft He definitely would become a great man and help him govern the country.

ref	mission:43						
tx	Nghĩ	vậy,	nh	vua	liền	phong	tước
mg	think	thus	respected	King	actˆimmediately	appoint	title
gu	V	DM	[GC]	N	[V]	V	N

tx	*Quan*	*Cận*		*Thần*	cho	*cậu.*
mg	mandarin	trusted^courtier	<		for/until	3s
gu	[GC]	N		<	CJ	KIN

ft Thus thinking, the king immediately gave him the title of Mandarin.

Son Tinh and Thuy Tinh
As told by Trần Văn Diến and Trần Cảnh Xuân (1993)

In the mythical story of *Son Tinh and Thuy Tinh,* two deities are personified as two young men. Son Tinh is the Mountain Spirit, and Thuy Tinh is the Sea Spirit. The two young men come to the court of the king and queen at the same time to ask for marriage to the princess, Mi Nuong. Because the young men are equally acceptable, the king cannot choose between the two of them. Therefore, he tells them to return the next day with wedding gifts, and whoever arrives first will be married to Mi Nuong. Son Tinh, the Mountain Spirit, arrives with his finery first and takes Mi Nuong to his mountain kingdom. Later Thuy Tinh, the Sea Spirit, arrives and is furious that Mi Nuong has gone with the Mountain Spirit. In his anger, he incites a hurricane, and turns the sea creatures into soldiers, ordering them to pursue the Mountain Spirit and Mi Nuong. The Mountain Spirit repels the Sea Spirit's attack by turning the land animals on the mountain into soldiers. The Mountain Spirit wins, but the Sea Spirit never gives up the idea of stealing Mi Nuong. As a result, the Sea Spirit assaults the Mountain Spirit's and Mi Nuong's kingdom with damaging rain storms every year.

```
ref   tinh:1
tx    Ng y   xưa             vua    Hùng   Vương   có         một
mg    day    past/former     King   Hung   Vuong   possess    one/a
gu    GC     AJ              N      NAM    NAM     V          NU

tx    cô                con       g i l   công      chúa   Mị    Nương.
mg    young^woman       offspring  girl    be        princess <   Mi    Nuong
gu    KIN               GC         N       CP  N     <        NAM   NAM

ft    Once upon a time, Emperor Hung Vuong had a beautiful daugh-
      ter, Princess Mi Nuong.

ref   tinh:2
tx    Công      chúa   nổi    tiếng         l  đ p          khiến
mg    princess  <      rise   reputation    be be^beautiful cause
gu    N         <      [V]    GC            CP [SV]         V
```

tx	nhiều	ch ng	trai	c c	nước	đến	
mg	much/many	young^man	young^man	various	nation	come^to	
gu	QNF	KCL	N	PL	GC	[V]	

tx	cầu	hôn.
mg	be^eager^for	kiss
gu	SV	N

ft The princess was renowned for her beauty, causing many young men [from] various nations to come [and] propose marriage.

ref tinh:3

tx	Tuy	nhi n,	vua	Hùng	Vương	nghĩ	l	không	ai
mg	though	so	King	Hung	Vuong	think	be	not	anyone
gu	CJ	CJ	N	NAM	NAM	V	CP	NG	IDN

tx	xứng	với	con	g i	mình.
mg	worthy	for	offspring	girl	self
gu	AJ	[PRE]	GC	N	PRO

ft However, Emperor Hung Vuong did not think [there] was anyone worthy of his daughter.

ref tinh:4

tx	Ng i		muốn	Mị	Nương	phải	kết
mg	[his]excellency		want	Mi	Nuong	must	plait
gu	GC		V	NAM	NAM	MD	V

tx	duy n	với	người	n o	thật	lỗi	lạc
mg	predestined^union	for	person	which	be^genuine	blame	lose
gu	N	[PRE]	GC	DM	[SV]	N	V

tx	v	quyền	thế.
mg	and	power	vantage
gu	CJ	N	N

ft He wanted Mi Nuong to marry someone really distinguished and powerful.

ref   tinh:5

tx	Ho ng	hậu	cũng	rất	lo	lắng	cho	tương
mg	[royal]	empress	likewise	very	worry	settle	for/until	future
gu	[AJ]	N	PRT	AV	V	V	CJ	N

tx	lai	con	g i.
mg	come	offspring	girl
gu	V	GC	N

ft   The queen likewise was very much concerned for [her] daughter's future.

ref   tinh:6

tx	B	âu	yếm	nhìn	Mị	Nương	rồi	nói:
mg	madam	caress	<	look^at	Mi	Nuong	then	speak/say
gu	KIN	V	<	V	NAM	NAM	[AV]	V

tx	'Đã		tới	lúc	con		phải	lập
mg	[to^have^already]		arrive	moment	[your^child]		must	establish
gu	ASP		V	[GC]	KIN		MD	V

tx	gia	đình,		con	ạ!		M	
mg	extend	communal^house		[your^child]	yes[sir/ma'm]		mother	
gu	V	N		KIN	ITJ		KIN	

tx	hy	vọng	ba	con	sẽ	tìm	được	
mg	hope	<	papa	[your^child]	shall	seek	finish^successfully	
gu	V	<	KIN	KIN	[MD]	V	ASP	

tx	cho	con	một	người	xứng	đ ng.'	
mg	for/until	[your^child]	one/a	person	worthy	be^worthy	
gu	CJ	KIN	NU	GC	AJ	SV	

ft   She tenderly looked at Mi Nuong and said: "The time has come [for] you to start your family, darling! I hope your father will find a worthy man for you."

ref	tinh:7							
tx	Nghe	thế,	Công	chúa	bồi	hồi	cảm động, muốn khóc
mg	hear	so	princess	<	fret	<	feel move want cry
gu	V	CJ	N	<	V	<	V V V V

tx	vì	sung	sướng.
mg	because^of	full	carefree
gu	PRT	AJ	AJ

ft   Hearing this, the princess was moved with emotion [and] wanted to cry because [she was so] happy.

ref   tinh:8

tx	N ng	thưa	lại:	'C m ơn m
mg	damsel	reply^politely	moreover feel	< mother
gu	KCL	[V]	PRT V	< KIN

tx	đã	lo	lắng	cho	con.'
mg	[to^have^already]	worry	settle	for/until	[your^child]
gu	ASP	V	V	CJ	KIN

ft   The young lady then replied respectfully, "Thank you, mother, [for] being concerned for me."

ref   tinh:9

tx	Việc	ấy	con	xin	để	tuỳ
mg	concern	that	[your^child]	request	for	do^in^accordance^with
gu	N	DM	KIN	V	[PRE]	V

tx	ba	m	định	liệu.
mg	papa	mother	intend	suit
gu	KIN	KIN	V	V

ft   "I want you and papa to do as [you] see fit concerning this."

ref	tinh:10						
tx	Vâng,	con	cũng	hiểu	con		phải
mg	Okay	[your^child]	likewise	understand	[your^child]		must
gu	[FW]	KIN	PRT	V	KIN		MD

tx	lập	gia	đình	v	sinh	con
mg	establish	extend	communal^house	and	give^birth^to	offspring
gu	V	V	N	CJ	V	GC

tx	để		c i	như	những	người	đ n
mg	give^birth^to		first^born	like	[PLURAL]	person	[HONORIFIC]
gu	V		N	PRT	PL	GC	KIN

tx	b	kh c.
mg	madam	other
gu	KIN	AJ

ft   "Yes, I likewise understand I must start a family and bear [my] first child like other women."

ref	tinh:11						
tx	Con	tin	ba	con	sẽ	chọn	cho
mg	[your^child]	believe	papa	[your^child]	shall	choose	for/until
gu	KIN	V	KIN	KIN	[MD]	V	CJ

tx	con	một	người	như	ý.
mg	[your^child]	one/a	person	like	mind
gu	KIN	NU	GC	[SV]	N

ft   "I believe my papa will choose a suitable person for me."

ref	tinh:12							
tx	Một	hôm	có	hai	ch ng	thanh	ni n	xuất
mg	one/a	afternoon	exist	two	young^man	youth	<	go^out
gu	NU	GC	V	NU	KCL	N>	<	[V]

tx	hiện.
mg	appear
gu	V

ft One day, there appeared two young men.

ref tinh:13

tx	Một	ch ng	t n	l	Sơn	Tinh,	thần	núi.
mg	one/a	young^man	name	be	Son	Tinh	diety	mountain
gu	NU	KCL	N	CP	NAM	NAM	N	N

ft One young man was named Son Tinh, the Mountain Spirit,

ref tinh:14

tx	Ch ng	kia	l	Thủy	Tinh,	thần	biển.
mg	young^man	other	be	Thuy	Tinh	diety	sea
gu	KCL	AJ	CP	NAM	NAM	N	N

ft [and] the other young man was Thuy Tinh, the Sea Spirit.

ref tinh:15

tx	Cả	hai	đều	đ p	trai,	lỗi	lạc
mg	all/the^whole	two	equally	be^beautiful	young^man	blame	lose
gu	PRT	NU	AUX	[SV]	N	N	V

tx	v	quyền	lực	như nhau.
mg	and	power	force	like each^other
gu	CJ	N	N	[SV] PRT

ft Both [were] equally handsome, distinguished, and powerful.

ref tinh:16

tx	Chỉ	kh c	nhau	ở	t nh
mg	only/just	other	each^other	have^certain^habits	disposition
gu	PRT	AJ	PRT	V	N

tx	tình.
mg	emotion
gu	N

ft   Only, [they] each had a certain character.

ref   tinh:17

tx	Sơn	Tinh	thuỳ		mị	v	trầm	tĩnh.
mg	Son	Tinh	sweet/gentle		charming	and	sluggish	quiet
gu	NAM	NAM	AJ		AJ	CJ	AJ	AJ

ft   Son Tinh [was] gentle and calm.

ref   tinh:18

tx	Thủy	Tinh	tr i	lại,		rất	nóng
mg	Thuy	Tinh	contrary	act^contrary^to^expected		very	quick/hot
gu	NAM	NAM	AJ	V		AV	AJ

tx	nảy.
mg	flash
gu	V

ft   Thuy Tinh, on the contrary, [was] very hot-tempered.

ref   tinh:19

tx	Sơn	Tinh	lễ	phép	cúi	đầu	tâu:
mg	Son	Tinh	politeness	permission	bow	head	address[king]
gu	NAM	NAM	N	N	V	N	V

tx	Con	t n	l	Sơn	Tinh,	trị	vì	
mg	[your^child]	name	be	Son	Tinh	govern	for^the^sake^of	
gu	KIN	N	CP	NAM	NAM	V	CJ	

tx	khắp	núi	rừng	v	cai	quản	c c
mg	everywhere/all	mountain	forest	and	manage	manage	various
gu	AJ	N	N	CJ	V	V	PL

tx	sinh	vật	sống		trn	núi.
mg	give^birth^to	creature	complete/whole		on/upon	mountain
gu	V	N	AJ		RN	N

ft Son Tinh respectfully bowed [his] head, addressing [the Emperor]: "My name is Son Tinh; [I] reign over all the forested mountains and manage the various living things in all the mountains."

ref tinh:20

tx	Tất	cả	kho	tng trn		núi,
mg	all/the^whole	all/the^whole	storehouse	hide on/upon		mountain
gu	PRT	PRT	N	V RN		N

tx	cây cỏ,		hoa	l	đều	l của		con.
mg	tree grass/weed		flower	leaf	equally	be possession		[your^child]
gu	[GC] N		N	N	AUX	CP GC		KIN

ft "All the treasures on the mountains, including the trees, flowers, [and] plants, are my possessions."

ref tinh:21

tx	Con	có	thế	tập	hợp	sư tử	<	v
mg	[your^child]	possess	vantage	assemble	gather	lion	<	and
gu	KIN	V	N	V	V	N	<	CJ

tx	chim muông.
mg	bird quadraped
gu	N N

ft "I can summon lions and birds [and] beasts."

ref tinh:22

tx	Con	cũng	l m	được	cho	núi		cao
mg	[your^child]	likewise	cause	be^able^to	cause	mountain		be^high
gu	KIN	PRT	V	ASP	V	N		[SV]

tx	lên	tận	trời.					
mg	go^up	as^far^as	sky					
gu	[V]	CJ	GC					

ft "I also can make the mountains grow as high as the sky."

ref tinh:23

tx	Con	xin	kết	hôn	cùng	Công	Chúa	v	hứa
mg	[your^child]	request	plait	kiss	with	princess	<		and	promise
gu	KIN	V	V	N	[V]	N	<	CJ	V

tx	đem	lại	cho	n ng	hạnh
mg	take/bring	again	for/until	damsel	good^nature
gu	V	[AV]	CJ	KCL	N

tx	phúc	v	cuộc	sống	bất	tử.
mg	blessing/happiness	and	existence	be^alive	without	<
gu	N	CJ	MC	[SV]	[AJ]	<

ft "I want to marry the princess and promise to bring her happiness and an eternal life."

ref tinh:24

tx	Đến	lượt	Thủy	Tinh	tiến	l n,	cúi	đầu
mg	come^to	turn	Thuy	Tinh	advance	go^up	bow	head
gu	[V]	N	NAM	NAM	[V]	[V]	V	N

tx	tâu:	T n	con	l	Thủy	Tinh.
mg	address[king]	name	[your^child]	be	Thuy	Tinh
gu	V	N	KIN	CP	NAM	NAM

ft [When it] came to Thuy Tinh's turn, [he] stepped forward, bowing [his] head [to the king], "My name is Thuy Tinh."

ref tinh:25

tx	Con	l m	chủ	c c	vật	sống	dưới
mg	[your^child]	be	master	various	creature	be^alive	below/under
gu	KIN	CP	N	PL	N	[SV]	RN

```
tx    nước.
mg    water
gu    N
```

ft   "I am master [of] the various creatures living under the water."

```
ref   tinh:26
tx    C c       giống  san    hô,  ngọc trai   v    kho         t ng
mg    various  strain coral  <    gem  oyster and  storehouse  hide
gu    PL       [GC]   N      <    N    N      CJ   N           V

tx    dưới         đ y     biển đều      l    của         con.
mg    below/under  bottom  sea  equally  be   possession  [your^child]
gu    RN           N       N    AUX      CP   GC          KIN
```

ft   "All the various strains of coral, pearls, and treasures under the sea are my possessions."

```
ref   tinh:27
tx    Con           l m    được          cho    mặt     biển dâng   l n
mg    [your^child]  cause  be^able^to    cause  surface sea  rise   go^up
gu    KIN           V      ASP           V      N       N    [V]    [V]

tx    tận         đỉnh  núi.
mg    as^far^as   top   mountain
gu    CJ          N     N
```

ft   "I can make the surface of the sea rise as high as the mountain top."

```
ref   tinh:28
tx    Con           có        thế      gây       ra       mưa   bão.
mg    [your^child]  possess   vantage  provoke   go^out   rain  storm
gu    KIN           V         N        V         [V]      N     N
```

ft   "I can gather rain storms."

Four Vietnamese Narrative Texts   171

ref   tinh:29

tx   Nếu   Công   Chúa   bằng   lòng   kết   hôn   với   con,
mg   if   princess <   even/level   heart   plait kiss with   [your^child]
gu   CJ   N   <   RN   N   V   N   [V]   KIN

tx   n ng   sẽ   trở   thanh nữ   ho ng   của
mg   damsel   shall   become   <   woman [royal] possession
gu   KCL   [MD]   V   <   N   [AJ]   GC

tx   đại   dương.
mg   enormous   ocean
gu   AJ   N

ft   "If the princess [is] content to marry me, she will become the queen of the ocean."

ref   tinh:30

tx   Cả   c i   thế   giới   tuyệt   vời
mg   all/the^whole   one^thing   world   kingdom   excellent very
gu   PRT   MC   N   N   AJ   AV

tx   dưới   đ y   biển v   thuỷ   cung   tr ng
mg   below/under   bottom   sea and   water   palace   magnificent
gu   RN   N   N   CJ   N   N   AJ

tx   lệ   sẽ   thuộc   về   n ng.
mg   beautiful   shall   belong   belong   damsel
gu   AJ   [MD]   V   V   KCL

ft   "The whole undersea world and the magnificent water palace will belong to her."

ref   tinh:31

tx   Nh   vua   lắng   tai   nghe.
mg   respected   King   listen^closely   ear   hear
gu   [GC]   N   V   N   V

ft   The emperor listened attentively.

| ref | tinh:32 |

tx	Ng i	bối	rối	không	biết	chọn
mg	[his]excellency	[beˆembarrassed] <	not	know	choose
gu	GC	[SV] <	NG	V	V

tx	ai,	vì	cả	hai	đều	đến	cùng
mg	anyone	becauseˆof	all/theˆwhole	two	equally	comeˆto	same
gu	IDN	PRT	PRT	NU	AUX	[V]	AJ

tx	một	lúc,	lại	đ p	trai	v	quyền
mg	one/a	moment	moreover	beˆbeautiful	youngˆman	and	power
gu	NU	[GC]	PRT	[SV]	N	CJ	N

tx	lực	như nhau.
mg	force	like eachˆother
gu	N	[SV] PRT

ft   He was embarrassed [and] did not know [how to] choose one because both [had] arrived at the same moment; moreover, one young man [was] equally as handsome and powerful as the other.

| ref | tinh:33 |

tx	Sau	cùng,	ng i	bảo	họ:	Ng y	mai,
mg	placeˆbehind	follow	[his]excellency	say	3p	day	tomorrow
gu	RN	[V]	GC	V	PRO	GC	N

tx	ai	đưa	s nh	lễ	tới	trước,
mg	anyone	putˆforward	[weddingˆpresents]	politeness	arrive	ahead
gu	IDN	V	N	N	V	RN

tx	ta	sẽ	gả	Công	chúa	cho.
mg	1sˆSUP	shall	giveˆforˆmarriage	princess <		forˆbenefitˆof
gu	PRO	[MD]	V	N	<	PRT

ft   Afterwards, he said to them: "Tomorrow whoever brings the wedding gifts first, I will give the princess to [him] to marry."

ref	tinh:34								
tx	Hai	chàng	vội	vã	ra	về	với	hy	vọng
mg	two	young^man	hasten	go^on^foot	exit	return	with	hope	<
gu	NU	KCL	V	<	V	[V]	[V]	V	<

tx	sẽ	cưới	được	Công	chúa.
mg	shall	marry	be^able^to	princess	<
gu	[MD]	V	ASP	N	<

ft The two young men hurried back out, in the hope of being able to marry the princess.

ref	tinh:35							
tx	Thủy	Tinh	sai	người	đi	mò	ngọc trai,	châu
mg	Thuy	Tinh	command	person	go	fish^for	gem oyster	pearl
gu	NAM	NAM	V	GC	V	V	N N	N

tx	báu	và	những	đồ	biển	ngon	lành,
mg	precious	and	[PLURAL]	thing	sea	tasty	wholesome
gu	AJ	CJ	PL	[MC]	N	AJ	AJ

tx	qúi		gi		nhất.
mg	be^noble/precious		valued/worth		most/best
gu	[SV]		GC		AJ

ft Thuy Tinh commanded [his] people to fish for the most precious pearls, the most valuable jewelry, and the most delicious seafood.

ref	tinh:36						
tx	Sơn	Tinh	mau	mắn	trở	về	núi,	ra
mg	Son	Tinh	be^quick	<	return	return	mountain	go^out
gu	NAM	NAM	V	<	[V]	[V]	N	[V]

tx	lệnh	cho	các	thuộc	hạ	tìm	kiếm
mg	decree	for/until	various	be^under	beneath	seek	try^to^find
gu	N	CJ	PL	SV	PRE	V	V

tx	hột	xo n,	cẩm		thạch	to n những	thứ
mg	stone/pit	diamond	bright/beautiful		stone	all [PLURAL]	sort
gu	N	N	AJ		N	[AV] PL	MC

tx	hảo	hạng.
mg	high^grade	class/rank
gu	AJ	[GC]

ft Son Tinh promptly returned to the mountain, [and] gave the command for [his] subordinates to try to find diamonds [and] stones of the highest quality.

ref tinh:37

tx	Ch ng	cũng	lựa	chọn	c c	giống hoa
mg	young^man	likewise	select	choose	various	strain flower
gu	KCL	PRT	V	V	PL	[GC] N

tx	thơm,	quả	ngọt	đem	dâng		vua	v
mg	fragrant	fruit	tasty	take/bring	offer^respectfully		King	and
gu	AJ	GC	AJ	V	V		N	CJ

tx	Ho ng	Hậu.
mg	royal	empress
gu	AJ	N

ft The young man also selected various fragrant flowers [and] tasty fruit to bring [and] offer respectfully to the emperor and the empress.

ref tinh:38

tx	S ng	hôm	sau,	Sơn	Tinh	tới	trước.
mg	morning	day	place^behind	Son	Tinh	arrive	ahead
gu	N	GC	RN	NAM	NAM	V	RN

ft The next morning, Son Tinh arrived first.

ref	tinh:39						
tx	Đi	theo	ch ng	có cả	trăm	người	
mg	go	with	young^man	be all/the^whole	hundred	person	
gu	V	[V]	KCL	CP PRT	NU	GC	

tx	mang	những	mâm đầy	châu b u,	những
mg	carry^with^one	[PLURAL]	tray full^of	pearl precious	[PLURAL]
gu	V	PL	N QNF	N AJ	PL

tx	rổ	xo i,		nho,	dâu	tây,	hồng,	lan	v.v...
mg	basket	arrayed^on^ground		grape	berry	west	rose	orchid	etc.
gu	N	AJ		N	N	AJ	N	N	ABB

ft With the young man were a hundred persons carrying trays full of valuables, [and] baskets arrayed on the ground with grapes, strawberries, roses, orchids, etc.

ref	tinh:40						
tx	Lễ	vật	khiến	nh	vua	ưng	ý	lắm,
mg	politeness	thing	cause	respected	King	accept	mind	much/many
gu	N	N	V	[GC]	N	V	N	PRT

tx	Ng i	bằng	lòng	gả	con
mg	[his]excellency	even/level	heart	give^for^marriage	offspring
gu	GC	RN	N	V	GC

tx	g i	cho	Sơn	Tinh.
mg	girl	for/until	Son	Tinh
gu	N	CJ	NAM	NAM

ft The offerings caused the king to be very satisfied, [and] he was content to give his daughter in marriage to Son Tinh.

ref	tinh:41							
tx	Mị	Nương	từ	gĩa	cha	m	rồi	bước l n
mg	Mi	Nuong	say^goodbye^to	<	father	mother	then	step go^up
gu	NAM	NAM	V	<	KIN	KIN	[AV]	V [V]

tx	*xe*	*hoa*	*theo*	*Sơn*	*Tinh*	*về*	*núi.*	
mg	vehicle	<	with	Son	Tinh	return	mountain	
gu	N	<	[V]	NAM	NAM	[V]	N	

ft Mi Nuong bid farewell to [her] parents, then stepped into the palaquin with Son Tinh to return to the mountain.

ref tinh:42

tx	*Sơn*	*Tinh*	*v*	*Mị*	*Nương*	*vừa*	*ra*	*khỏi*	*cung*	*điện*
mg	Son	Tinh	and	Mi	Nuong	just^now	exit	escape	palace	court
gu	NAM	NAM	CJ	NAM	NAM	AV	V	V	N	N

tx	*thì*	*Thủy*	*Tinh*	*v*	*đo*	*n*	*tùy*	*tùng*	*tới,*
mg	then	Thuy	Tinh	and	delegation		escort	follow	arrive
gu	PRT	NAM	NAM	CJ	N		V	[V]	V

tx	*mang*		*theo*	*ngọc*	*trai,*	*nữ*	*trang*	*v*	*c*	*c*
mg	carry^with^one		with	gem	oyster	jewelry	trousseau	and	various
gu	V		[V]	N	N	N	N	CJ	PL

tx	*thứ*	*đồ*	*biển.*
mg	sort	thing	sea
gu	MC	[MC]	N

ft Son Tinh and Mi Nuong had just escaped from the palace court when Thuy Tinh and [his] delegation arrived, carrying with them pearls, jewelry, and various sea products.

ref tinh:43

tx	*Khi*	*biết*	*Mị*	*Nương*	*đã*	*ra*	*đi*	*với*
mg	when	realize	Mi	Nuong	[to^have^already]	go^out	go	with
gu	GC	V	NAM	NAM	ASP	[V]	V	[V]

tx	*Sơn*	*Tinh*	*mấy*	*phút*	*trước,*	*Thủy*	*Tinh*	*nổi*
mg	Son	Tinh	some	minute/moment	ahead	Thuy	Tinh	rise
gu	NAM	NAM	IDN	GC	RN	NAM	NAM	[V]

tx	*giận*	*đùng*	*đùng.*	
mg	be^angry	suddenly	suddenly	
gu	SV	AV	AV	
ft	When [he] realized Mi Nuong had gone with Son Tinh some minutes before, Thuy Tinh flew into a passion [and] exploded with fury.			

ref	tinh:44						
tx	*Chàng*	*liền*		*truyền*	*cho*	*gia*	*nhân*
mg	young^man	act^immediately		order	for/until	family	human
gu	KCL	[V]		V	CJ	N	N

tx	*đuổi*	*theo*	*Sơn*	*Tinh,*	*mong*	*bắt*	*Mị*	*Nương lại.*
mg	pursue	with	Son	Tinh	wait^eagerly	sieze	Mi	Nuong again
gu	V	[V]	NAM	NAM	V	V	NAM	NAM [AV]

ft The young man immediately ordered [his] servants to pursue Son Tinh, [and] wait [for a chance to] seize Mi Nuong again.

ref tinh:45

tx	*Thủy*	*Tinh*	*vừa*	*hò*	*hét*	*vừa*	*vung*	*chiếc*
mg	Thuy	Tinh	just^now	call^out	shriek	just^now	flourish	unit^of
gu	NAM	NAM	AV	V	V	AV	V	MC

tx	*gươm*	*thần.*
mg	sword	magic
gu	N	AJ

ft Thuy Tinh shouted and flourished his magic sword.

ref tinh:46

tx	*Tức*	*thì*	*các*		*sinh*	*vật*	*dưới*	*biển*
mg	presently	then	various		give^birth^to	creature	below/under	sea
gu	AV	PRT	PL		V	N	RN	N

tx	*biến*	*th nh*	*ng n*	*vạn*	*quân*	*binh.*
mg	disappear	turn^into	thousand	ten^thousand	army	soldier
gu	V	V	NU	NU	[MC]	N

ft Instantly the various undersea creatures turned into thousands of soldiers.

ref tinh:47

tx	*Trời*	*bắt*	*đầu*	*mưa*	*to*	*gió*	*lớn.*
mg	sky	start	beginning	rain	big	wind	big
gu	GC	V	N	V	AJ	N	AJ

ft The sky began [to let loose] heavy rain [and] strong winds.

ref tinh:48

tx	*Nước*	*dâng*	*l n*	*mỗi*	*lúc*	*một*	*cao.*
mg	water	rise	go^up	each	moment	one/a	be^high
gu	N	[V]	[V]	PL	[GC]	NU	[SV]

ft The water rose up higher each moment.

ref tinh:49

tx	*Nh*	*cửa,*	*cây cối*	*bị*	*sóng*	*đ nh,*
mg	dwelling	belongings	tree [shrubbery]	[NEG^PASS]	wave	catch
gu	N	N	[GC] N	ASP	N	V

tx	*cuốn*	*trôi*	*theo*	*dòng*	*nước*	*lũ.*
mg	carry^away	be^afloat	with	flow	water	heavy^rain
gu	V	SV	[V]	N	N	N

ft Dwellings [and] trees were caught by the waves, carried afloat with the flow of heavy rainwater.

ref   tinh:50

tx   *Sơn Tinh cũng có cây gậy thần.*
mg   Son Tinh likewise possess tree stick/cane magic
gu   NAM NAM PRT V [GC] N AJ

ft   Son Tinh likewise had a magic wand.

ref   tinh:51

tx   *Ch ng hóa phép cho những*
mg   young^man change^into magic^trick cause [PLURAL]
gu   KCL V N V PL

tx   *lo i vật tr n núi trở th nh*
mg   species/kind creature on/upon mountain become turn^into
gu   GC N RN N V V

tx   *ng n vạn quân binh để phản công.*
mg   thousand ten^thousand army soldier for oppose attack
gu   NU NU [MC] N [PRE] V V

ft   The young man made the animals on the mountain turn into thousands of soldiers to fight back.

ref   tinh:52

tx   *Nước c ng dâng l n, Sơn Tinh c ng*
mg   water more^and^more rise go^up Son Tinh more^and^more
gu   N AUX [V] [V] NAM NAM AUX

tx   *l m cho núi cao th m.*
mg   cause for/until mountain be^high add
gu   V CJ N [SV] [V]

ft   The more the water rose, the more Son Tinh caused the mountain to rise.

ref	tinh:53								
tx	Cuộc	chiến	giữa		Sơn	Tinh	v	Thủy Tinh	kéo d i
mg	bout	war	place^between		Son	Tinh	and	Thuy Tinh	pull long
gu	MC	N	RN		NAM	NAM	CJ	NAM NAM	V AJ

tx	nhiều	ng y.
mg	much/many	day
gu	QNF	GC

ft The war between Son Tinh and Thuy Tinh drew on [for] many days.

ref	tinh:54			
tx	Không	b n	n o	thắng.
mg	not	side	which	win
gu	NG	[N]	DM	V

ft [There was] no side which won.

ref	tinh:55				
tx	Nhiều	người	bị	thiệt	mạng.
mg	much/many	person	[NEG^PASS]	suffer^loss	life
gu	QNF	GC	ASP	V	N

ft Many people lost their lives.

ref	tinh:56					
tx	Sau	cùng,	phe		Thủy	Tinh thua,
mg	place^behind	the^end	faction/camp		Thuy	Tinh be^defeated
gu	RN	N	N		NAM	NAM V

tx	rút	xuống	biển.
mg	withdraw	go^down	sea
gu	V	V	N

ft Finally, Thuy Tinh's faction were defeated [and] withdrew down [to] the sea.

ref tinh:57

tx	Tuy	vậy,	Thủy	Tinh	không	từ		bỏ	ý
mg	though	so	Thuy	Tinh	not	say^goodbye^to		leave	mind
gu	CJ	DM	NAM	NAM	NG	V		V	N

tx	định	cướp	lại	công	chúa.
mg	intend	snatch	again	princess	<
gu	V	V	[AV]	N	<

ft However, Thuy Tinh did not say goodbye to [his] intention of snatching the princess again.

ref tinh:58

tx	Năm	n o	Thủy	Tinh	cũng	l m	nước	dâng	cao
mg	year	each/every	Thuy	Tinh	even	cause	water	rise	be^high
gu	GC	AJ	NAM	NAM	[AV]	V	N	[V]	[SV]

tx	v	gây	bão	gió	tr n	đỉnh	núi	nơi	Sơn
mg	and	provoke	storm	wind	on/upon	top	mountain	place	Son
gu	CJ	V	N	N	RN	N	N	N	NAM

tx	Tinh	v	Mị	Nương	chung	sống,	nhưng	chẳng		bao
mg	Tinh	and	Mi	Nuong	share	be^alive	but	not^at^all		ever
gu	NAM	CJ	NAM	NAM	V	[SV]	PRT	NG		DM

tx	giờ	thắng.
mg	time	win
gu	GC	V

ft Every year Thuy Tinh even causes the water to rise high and gathers wind [and] storms on the mountain top where Son Tinh and Mi Nuong share their lives, but [he] never ever wins.

ref tinh:59

tx	Mỗi	khi	trận	chiến	bùng	nổ	giữa		Sơn
mg	each	when	struggle	war	flare^up	burst	place^between		Son
gu	PL	GC	N	N	V	V	RN		NAM

tx	*Tinh*	*v*	*Thủy*	*Tinh*	*thi*	*dân*	*chúng*	*khổ*
mg	Tinh	and	Thuy	Tinh	compete	subject/citizen	people	miserable
gu	NAM	CJ	NAM	NAM	V	N	[QNF]	[SV]

tx	*sở,*	*lo i*	*vật*	*bị*	*chết chóc,*	
mg	miserable	species/kind	creature	[NEG^PASS]	die	<
gu	[AJ]	GC	N	ASP	V	<

tx	*mùa*	*m ng*	*của*	*cải bị*	*hư*	
mg	crop/season	<	possession	<	[NEG^PASS]	damaged
gu	GC	<	GC	<	ASP	AJ

tx	*hại.*
mg	harm/damage
gu	V

ft   Each time the war breaks out between Son Tinh and Thuy Tinh, people are in misery, animals are killed, crops and property are damaged.

The Story of the Mosquito
As told by Trần Văn Diến and L Tinh Thông (1992)

The Story of the Mosquito is a myth that explains why mosquitos bite. The legend begins with a destitute young couple living in a small village. The husband is a scholar, and the wife is a beautiful woman who loves her husband deeply. However, the wife has an insatiable desire for wealth and luxury that eventually causes her to waste away. Her husband refuses to accept her death and will not bury her. He travels around the countryside, looking for a diety to bring her back to life. Finally, he finds an old, wise man who instructs him to go to his wife's bedside, bite his own finger, then place two droplets of his blood on his wife's lips. The husband does this and his wife comes back to life. However, she still longs for luxury and hates the way she and her husband live. A rich man of high social status comes to their village and builds a sumptuous house next to the young couple's hovel. He is attracted to the wife by her beauty, seduces her with his wealth, and she eventually goes to live with him. The heartbroken husband begs his wife to come home, but she refuses. At last, the husband confronts his wife with the fact that she has been ungrateful to him. The indignant wife bites her finger to return the two droplets of blood to her husband, but the blood does not reach him; it drops to the ground. When this happens, she turns into a mosquito, forever damned to hunt for those two, life-giving droplets of blood.

ref   mosquito:1

tx	Ng y	xưa	tại	một	ngôi	l ng	nhỏ	có
mg	day	past/former	be^at/in	one/a	house	village	small	exist
gu	GC	AJ	[SV]	NU	[MC]	GC	AJ	V

tx	hai	vợ	chồng	trẻ	sống	trong	một	căn	nh
mg	two	wife	husband	young	be^alive	within	one/a	house	dwelling
gu	NU	N	N	[SV]	[SV]	[PRE]	NU	[GC]	N

tx	chật	h p.
mg	cramped	narrow
gu	AJ	AJ

ft   Once upon a time in a small village there was a young couple living in a cramped house.

ref   mosquito:2

tx   *Người   chồng   rất   tốt.*
mg   person husband very   good
gu   GC   N   AV   AJ

ft   The husband was very good.

ref   mosquito:3

tx   *Anh   l   một   học   giả   suốt*
mg   close^male^relative be   one/a learn [AGENTIVE]   throughout
gu   KIN   CP   NU   V   AGM   CJ

tx   *ng y chỉ   th ch   nghiền   ng m   s ch   vở.*
mg   day only/just be^fond^of learn^thoroughly ponder   book   <
gu   GC PRT   V   V   V   N   GC

ft   He was a scholar, [and] was fond of just pondering books all day.

ref   mosquito:4

tx   *Nhưng   anh   lại   rất   nghèo.*
mg   but/yet close^male^relative moreover   very   poor
gu   CJ   KIN   PRT   AV   AJ

ft   But he was also very poor.

ref   mosquito:5

tx   *Con   vợ   anh   l   một   người   đ n*
mg   Young   wife   close^male^relative be   one/a person   [HONORIFIC]
gu   KIN   N   KIN   CP   NU   GC   KIN

tx   *b   có nhan sắc   v   y u   chồng*
mg   madam   be face women's^appearance   and love   husband
gu   KIN   CP N   N   CJ   V   N

tx	*tha*	*thiết.*	
mg	have^consideration	care^for	
gu	V	V	

ft His young wife was a woman who was beautiful and [who] loved [her] husband deeply.

ref mosquito:6

tx	*Nhưng*	*n ng*	*lại*	*th ch*	*ăn*
mg	but/yet	damsel	act^contrary^to^expected	be^fond^of	receive
gu	CJ	KCL	V	V	V

tx	*sang*	*mặc*	*đ p.*
mg	expensive/luxurious	wear	be^beautiful
gu	AJ	V	[SV]

ft But she was fond of getting expensive [and] beautiful [things] to wear.

ref mosquito:7

tx	*N ng*	*luôn*	*luôn*	*mơ*	*ước*	*có*
mg	damsel	continuously	continuously	dream/wish	wish	possess
gu	KCL	AV	AV	V	V	V

tx	*một*	*căn*	*nh*	*thật*	*đ p,*	*v*
mg	one/a	house	dwelling	actual/true	be^beautiful	and
gu	NU	[GC]	N	AJ	[SV]	CJ

tx	*kẻ*	*hầu*	*người*	*hạ.*
mg	person/individual	attend/wait^upon	person	lower
gu	[GC]	V	GC	AJ

ft She incessantly wished to have a really beautiful house and servant(s).

ref mosquito:8

tx   N ng   không ưa   cuộc   sống   nghèo n n hiện
mg   damsel   not   like   existence beˆalive poor   <   atˆpresent
gu   KCL   NG   V   MC   [SV]   AJ   <   AV

tx   tại   của   mình.
mg   beˆat/in   possession   self
gu   [SV]   GC   PRO

ft   She did not like her own present, destitute existence.

ref mosquito:9

tx   N ng   không th ch   l m   những   công   việc nội
mg   damsel   not   beˆfondˆof   do/make   [PLURAL]   labor job   within
gu   KCL   NG   V   V   PL   N   N   [PRE]

tx   trợ   v   sinh   ch n   nản
mg   <   and   giveˆbirthˆto   beˆtiredˆof   beˆdiscouraged
gu   <   CJ   V   [SV]   SV

tx   buồn   phiền   đến   độ   mất   ăn
mg   sad/melancholy   worry   comeˆto   measure/timeˆperiod   lose eat
gu   [SV]   V   [V]   [GC]   V   V

tx   mất ngủ.
mg   lose sleep
gu   V   V

ft   She did not like to do housekeeping work and became disheartened to the point of not eating, [and] losing sleep.

ref mosquito:10

tx   Sức   khỏe   n ng   suy   giảm.
mg   strength   healthy   damsel   decline   reduce
gu   N   AJ   KCL   V   V

ft   Her health deteriorated.

```
ref   mosquito:11

tx    Chẳng      bao          lâu           n ng      ngã          bệnh
mg    not^at^all so^much/many long^while    damsel    fall^down    illness
gu    NG         DM           N             KCL       V            N

tx    nặng.
mg    serious
gu    AJ

ft    Very soon she fell seriously ill.

ref   mosquito:12

tx    C c      thầy    lang         y          cũng   đ nh
mg    various  master  herb^doctor  medicine   even   resign^self^to
gu    PL       N       N            N          [AV]   V

tx    bó        tay   không  chữa   được.
mg    give^up   <     not    cure   be^able^to
gu    V         <     NG     V      ASP

ft    Even the doctors gave up, unable to cure [her].

ref   mosquito:13

tx    Cuối        cùng        n ng      qua        đời.
mg    near^limit  the^end     damsel    pass^by    life
gu    AV          N           KCL       V          N

ft    Finally, she died.

ref   mosquito:14

tx    Người   chồng    buồn             rầu            v     nhớ    vợ
mg    person  husband  sad/melancholy   be^sorrowful   and   miss   wife
gu    GC      N        [SV]             AJ             CJ    V      N

tx    qu         đến       nỗi       nhất         định     không
mg    go^beyond  come^to   feeling   most/best    intend   not
gu    [V]        [V]       N         AJ           V        NG
```

tx	*chịu*		*cho*	*chôn*	*cất.*
mg	bring^oneself^to		allow	bury	<
gu	V		V	V	<

ft The husband was terribly sorrowful and missed [his] wife so much that [he] refused to bury [her].

ref mosquito:15

tx	*Anh*	*cầu*	*trời*	*khấn*	*Phật*
mg	close^male^relative	pray^to	heaven	whisper^prayers	Buddha
gu	KIN	V	GC	V	NAM

tx	*cho*	*vợ*	*mình*	*được*	*sống*	*lại.*
mg	for/until	wife	self	[PASSIVE]	be^alive	again
gu	CJ	N	PRO	ASP	[SV]	[AV]

ft He prayed to heaven, whispering prayers [to] Buddha for his wife to be brought to life again.

ref mosquito:16

tx	*Anh*	*quyết*	*tâm*	*đi*	*tìm*	*một*	*vị*
mg	close^male^relative	decide	[good]heart	go	seek	one/a	revered
gu	KIN	V	N	V	V	NU	[GC]

tx	*thần*	*để*	*xin*	*cứu*	*chữa.*
mg	diety	for	request	save/help	cure
gu	N	[PRE]	V	V	V

ft He was determined to go find a god [from which] to request a cure.

ref mosquito:17

tx	*Một*	*hôm*	*anh*	*gặp*	*một*	*ông*
mg	one/a	day	close^male^relative	encounter	one/a	male^relative
gu	NU	GC	KIN	V	NU	KIN

tx	gi	râu	tóc	bạc	phơ.
mg	old	beard	hair	hoary	snowy
gu	AJ	N	N	AJ	PRT

ft   One day he encountered an old man [with] a snowy white beard.

ref   mosquito:18

tx	Ông	gi	n y	nói		với	anh,
mg	gentleman	old	this	talk/tell		to	close^male^relative
gu	KIN	AJ	DM	V		[V]	KIN

tx	'Con	l	một	người	tốt	biết	tin	ở	trời.
mg	[your^child]	be	one/a	person	good	know	believe	in/at	heaven
gu	KIN	CP	NU	GC	AJ	V	V	[PRE]	GC

ft   This old man said to him, "You are a good, pious person."

ref   mosquito:19

tx	Vậy	giờ	đây	con	ước	muốn	điều	gì?'
mg	thus	time	this	[your^child]	wish	want	pretext	what?
gu	DM	GC	DM	KIN	V	V	N	IDN

ft   "So now what [is] it you wish?"

ref   mosquito:20

tx	Anh	liền	thưa	ngay,
mg	close^male^relative	act^immediately	reply^politely	immediately
gu	KIN	[V]	[V]	AV

tx	'Dạ	thưa	con	chỉ	xin	một
mg	[courteous]	reply^politely	[your^child]	only/just	request	one/a
gu	[FW]	PRT	KIN	PRT	V	NU

tx	*điều.*
mg	pretext
gu	N

ft He replied respectfully without hesitation, "Sir, I only request one thing."

ref mosquito:21

tx	*Đó*	*l*	*xin*	*cho*	*vợ*	*con*	*được*	*sống*
mg	that	be	request	for/until	wife	[your^child]	be^able^to	be^alive
gu	DM	CP	V	CJ	N	KIN	ASP	[SV]

tx	*lại.'*
mg	again
gu	[AV]

ft "That is a request that my wife be able to be alive again."

ref mosquito:22

tx	*Lão ông*	*suy*	*nghĩ*	*giây*	*l t*	*rồi*	*đ p,*
mg	old male^relative	consider	think	second	moment	then	reply
gu	AJ KIN	V	V	GC	[GC]	[AV]	V

tx	*'Con*	*hãy*	*trở*	*về*	*đến*	*b n*	*giường*	*vợ,*
mg	[your^child]	be^sure^to	return	return	come^to	side	bed	wife
gu	KIN	[MD]	[V]	[V]	[V]	[N]	N	N

tx	*rồi*	*cắn*	*ngón*	*tay*	*con*	*lấy*	*m u*	*nhỏ*	*hai*
mg	then	bite	finger	hand	[your^child]	take	blood	drop	two
gu	[AV]	V	[MC]	N	KIN	V	N	V	NU

tx	*giọt*	*l n*	*môi*	*vợ*	*con*	*thì*	*vợ*
mg	droplet	add^on	lip	wife	[your^child]	then	wife
gu	GC	V	N	N	KIN	PRT	N

tx	con	sẽ	sống	lại	ngay.'	
mg	[your^child]	shall	be^alive	again	immediately	
gu	KIN	[MD]	[SV]	[AV]	AV	

ft   The old man thought carefully for a few seconds, then replied, "You must return to [your] wife's bedside, then bite your finger [and] put two drops of blood on your wife's lips; then your wife will immediately be alive again."

ref   mosquito:23

tx	Anh	liền	c m	ơn	lão
mg	close^male^relative	act^immediately	appreciate	favor	old
gu	KIN	[V]	V	N	AJ

tx	ông	v	vội	v ng	trở	về	nh .
mg	male^relative	and	hasten	<	return	return	dwelling
gu	KIN	CJ	V	<	[V]	[V]	N

ft   He immediately thanked the old man and hastily returned home.

ref   mosquito:24

tx	Anh	l m	theo	lời	lão
mg	close^male^relative	do/make	with	spoken^words	old
gu	KIN	V	[V]	GC	AJ

tx	ông	căn dặn,		cắn	ngón	tay	v	nhỏ	hai
mg	male^relative	> recommend	bite	finger	hand	and	drop	two
gu	KIN	> V	V	[MC]	N	CJ	V	NU

tx	giọt	m u	l n	môi	vợ.
mg	droplet	blood	add^on	lip	wife
gu	GC	N	V	N	N

ft   He did as the old man had recommended, bit [his] finger and dropped two droplets of blood onto [his] wife's lips.

| ref | mosquito:25 |

tx	Bỗng	chốc	môi n ng		bắt	đầu	cử	động,
mg	act^suddenly	awhile	lip	damsel	start	beginning	move	move
gu	V	N	N	KCL	V	N	V	V

tx	rồi	đôi	mắt n ng		mở	ra.
mg	then	pair	eye	damsel	open	come^out
gu	[AV]	GC	N	KCL	V	V

ft Suddenly her lips began to move, then her eyes opened.

| ref | mosquito:26 |

tx	Thấy	vợ	mình	sống	lại,	anh
mg	perceive	wife	self	be^alive	again	close^male^relative
gu	V	N	PRO	[SV]	[AV]	KIN

tx	liền	qùi	xuống	tạ	ơn	Trời.
mg	act^immediately	kneel	go^down	thank	favor	heaven
gu	[V]	V	V	V	N	GC

ft Seeing his wife was alive again, he immediately knelt down to thank heaven.

| ref | mosquito:26a |

tx	Lòng	anh		vui	sướng	khôn	tả.
mg	heart	close^male^relative		pleased	carefree	impossible	describe
gu	N	KIN		SV	AJ	AJ	V

ft His heart was overwhelmed with joy.

| ref | mosquito:27 |

tx	Người	vợ	hiểu	rằng	mình	chết	chỉ	vì
mg	person	wife	understand	that	self	die	only/just	because^of
gu	GC	N	V	REL	PRO	V	PRT	PRT

Four Vietnamese Narrative Texts   193

tx	thiếu	hạng	phúc.	
mg	lack	class/rank	blessing/happiness	
gu	V	[GC]	N	

ft   The wife understood that she had died only because [she] lacked (socio-economic) class happiness.

ref mosquito:28

tx	N ng	cũng	biết	rằng	ch nh	chồng	mình
mg	damsel	likewise	realize	that	no^other^than	husband	self
gu	KCL	PRT	V	REL	AJ	N	PRO

tx	đã	l m	mình	sống	lại.
mg	[to^have^already]	cause	self	be^alive	again
gu	ASP	V	PRO	[SV]	[AV]

ft   She also realized that [it was] no other than her husband [that] had made her come back to life.

ref mosquito:29

tx	Nhưng	rồi	n ng	v n	không	thể	n o	chấp	nhận
mg	but/yet	then	damsel	still	not	may	which	accept	recognize
gu	CJ	[AV]	KCL	AUX	NG	MD	DM	V	V

tx	cuộc	sống	nghèo	n n	khổ	cực.
mg	existence	be^alive	poor	<	miserable	hard/suffering
gu	MC	[SV]	AJ	<	[SV]	AJ

ft   Yet, she still could not by any means comply with [their] miserable, destitute existence.

ref mosquito:30

tx	N ng	cố	sống	v	qu n	đi	những	mơ
mg	damsel	try	be^lively	and	forget	[EMPHATIC]	[PLURAL]	dream/wish
gu	KCL	V	[SV]	CJ	V	PRT	PL	V

tx	ước	cảnh	gi u	sang		phú	
mg	wish	situation	wealthy	expensive/luxurious		endow	
gu	V	N	AJ	AJ		V	

tx	qúi.
mg	be^noble/precious
gu	[SV]

ft   She tried to be cheerful and go ahead [and] forget [her] dreams for an upper class, rich situation.

ref   mosquito:31

tx	Một	hôm	có	ông	phú	hộ	dọn	đến
mg	one/a	day	be	male^relative	endow	household	move	come^to
gu	NU	GC	CP	KIN	V	N	V	[V]

tx	ngôi	l ng	vợ	chồng	anh		học	giả
mg	house	village	wife	husband	close^male^relative		learn	[AGENTIVE]
gu	[MC]	GC	N	N	KIN		V	AGM

tx	n y	đang	ở.
mg	this	be^in^process^of	live
gu	DM	ASP	V

ft   One day [there] was a rich man [who] moved to the village [where] this wife and [her] scholar husband were living.

ref   mosquito:32

tx	Ông	ta	cho	xây	một	căn	nh	
mg	gentleman	1s^SUP	cause	build	one/a	house	dwelling	
gu	KIN	PRO	V	V	NU	[GC]	N	

tx	sang		trọng	s t	cạnh	nh
mg	expensive/luxurious		elegant	be^very^close	edge	dwelling
gu	AJ		AJ	SV	GC	N

tx	*anh.*
mg	close^male^relative
gu	KIN

ft   He had a luxurious house built just beside the [scholar's] house.

ref mosquito:33

tx	*Ông*	*nh*	*gi u*	*đó*	*gặp*	*vợ*
mg	gentleman	dwelling	wealthy	that	encounter	wife
gu	KIN	N	AJ	DM	V	N

tx	*anh*		*rồi*	*đâm*	*say*	*m*
mg	close^male^relative		then	thrust	be^under^a^spell	be^infatuated
gu	KIN		[AV]	V	[SV]	[SV]

tx	*sắc*	*đ p*	*của*	*n ng.*
mg	women's^appearance	be^beautiful	possession	damsel
gu	N	[SV]	GC	KCL

ft   That man [from] the wealthy family encountered the [scholar]'s wife and immediately became infatuated with the glamour of [the woman].

ref mosquito:34

tx	*Ông*	*bèn*	*dụ*	*dỗ*	*n ng*	*bỏ*	*chồng*
mg	gentleman	immediately	entice	coax	damsel	leave	husband
gu	KIN	AV	V	V	KCL	V	N

tx	*đi*	*theo*	*mình.*
mg	go	with	self
gu	V	[V]	PRO

ft   He immediately enticed her to leave [her] husband to go with him.

ref   mosquito:35

tx   Lúc   đầu   n ng   một   mực   từ   chối.
mg   moment   beginning damsel   one/a   level renounce refuse
gu   [GC]   N   KCL   NU   N   V   V

ft   At the beginning she steadfastly refused.

ref   mosquito:36

tx   Ông   nh   gi u   lại   hứa   sẽ   cho
mg   gentleman dwelling wealthy   inˆreturn promise shall give
gu   KIN   N   AJ   [AV]   V   [MD]   V

tx   n ng   tất   cả   những   gì   n ng   muốn.
mg   damsel   all   all/theˆwhole [PLURAL] any/atˆall damsel   want
gu   KCL   [AV] PRT   PL   IDN   KCL   V

ft   The man [from] the wealthy family in return promised to give her all [and] anything she wanted.

ref   mosquito:37

tx   Thế rồi   không chống   trả   nổi   sự   c m
mg   so then   not   oppose giveˆback   beˆableˆto event   appreciate
gu   CJ [AV]   NG   V   V   ASP   [GC]   V

tx   dỗ   mãnh   liệt   đó,   n ng   đã   bỏ
mg   coax   fierce violent that   damsel   [toˆhaveˆalready]   leave
gu   V   AJ   AJ   DM   KCL   ASP   V

tx   chồng   đi   theo   ông   nh   gi u.
mg   husband go   with   maleˆrelative   dwelling wealthy
gu   N   V   [V]   KIN   N   AJ

ft   Finally she could not resist such vehement seduction, [and] she left [her] husband to go with the man [from] the rich family.

Four Vietnamese Narrative Texts

ref   mosquito:38

tx   *N ng   được   ăn   sang   mặc   đ p*
mg   damsel   [PASSIVE] receive expensive/luxurious   wear be^beautiful
gu   KCL   ASP   V   AJ   V   [SV]

tx   *theo ý   muốn, có   nhiều   đầy   tớ*
mg   with mind   want   possess   much/many servant <
gu   [V]   N   V   V   QNF   N   <

tx   *hầu   hạ.*
mg   attend/wait^upon   lower
gu   V   AJ

ft   She was given the expensive, beautiful [things] to wear that she wanted, [and] had many servants.

ref   mosquito:39

tx   *N ng   thấy   hạnh   phúc   tr n   trề.*
mg   damsel   perceive   good^nature   blessing/happiness   overflow   <
gu   KCL   V   N   N   V   <

ft   She felt overwhelmingly happy.

ref   mosquito:40

tx   *Nhưng   trong   khi   đó   anh   ch ng*
mg   but/yet within   when   then   close^male^relative   young^man
gu   CJ   [PRE]   GC   DM   KIN   KCL

tx   *học   giả   nghèo   buồn   lắm.*
mg   learn [AGENTIVE]   poor   sad/melancholy   much/many
gu   V   AGM   AJ   [SV]   PRT

ft   But meanwhile, the poor young scholar [was] very sad.

ref	mosquito:41

tx	Anh		theo	năn	nỉ	vợ	trở	về	với
mg	close^male^relative		with	entreat	<	wife	return	return	to
gu	KIN		[V]	V	<	N	[V]	[V]	[V]

tx	mình	nhưng	đều	bị		từ	chối.	
mg	self	but	equally	[NEG^PASS]		renounce	refuse	
gu	PRO	PRT	AUX	ASP		V	V	

ft He begged [his] wife to return to him, but was consistently refused.

ref	mosquito:42

tx	Cuối	cùng	bực tức		qu	anh
mg	near^limit	the^end	fret	get^angry	excessive	close^male^relative
gu	AV	N	V	V	AJ	KIN

tx	mới	mắng	vợ,	'Cô		thật	l	một
mg	[right^then]	scold	wife	young^woman		actual/true	be	one/a
gu	PRT	V	N	KIN		AJ	CP	NU

tx	hạng	đ n	b	mất	nết.
mg	class/rank	[HONORIFIC]	madam	lose	[good]habit
gu	[GC]	KIN	KIN	V	N

ft Finally, [feeling] extremely upset, he just scolded [his] wife, "You truly are a fine woman [who] has lost her grace."

ref	mosquito:43

tx	Tôi	y u	cô	tha		thiết,	cho
mg	1s	love	young^woman	have^consideration		care^for	give
gu	PRO	V	KIN	V		V	V

tx	cô	tất	cả	những	gì	tôi
mg	young^woman	all	all/the^whole	[PLURAL]	any/at^all	1s
gu	KIN	[AV]	PRT	PL	IDN	PRO

tx	có,	cả		đến	những	giọt	m u	của
mg	possess	all/theˆwhole		even	[PLURAL]	droplet	blood	possession
gu	V	PRT		[AV]	PL	GC	N	GC

tx	tôi	để	mang		sự	sống	lại	
mg	1s	inˆorderˆto	carryˆwithˆone		event	beˆalive	inˆreturn	
gu	PRO	CJ	V		[GC]	[SV]	[AV]	

tx	cho	cô.
mg	for/until	youngˆwoman
gu	CJ	KIN

ft "I loved you so much [that] I gave you all I had, even my blood, in order to bring you back to life."

ref mosquito:44

tx	Thế	m	cô		đã		phản
mg	so	asˆaˆresult	youngˆwoman		[toˆhaveˆalready]		oppose
gu	CJ	CJ	KIN		ASP		V

tx	bội		tôi.'
mg	actˆbehindˆanother'sˆback		1s
gu	V		PRO

ft "And you betrayed me."

ref mosquito:45

tx	Người	vợ	ngạo		nghễ		trả	
mg	person	wife	beˆcontemptuous		glanceˆsideways		giveˆback	
gu	GC	N	V		V		V	

tx	lời,		'Tôi	có	thể	trả	lại	những	giọt
mg	spokenˆwords		1s	be	may	giveˆback	inˆreturn	[PLURAL]	droplet
gu	GC		PRO	CP	MD	V	[AV]	PL	GC

tx	m u	đó	cho	anh		ngay	bây	giờ.'
mg	blood	that	give	close^male^relative		immediately	right^now	time
gu	N	DM	V	KIN		AV	DM	GC

ft   [His] wife haughtily replied, "I can give back the blood that you gave [me] right now!"

ref mosquito:46

tx	Nói	xong	n ng		cắn	ngón	tay	mình.
mg	talk/tell	finish	damsel		bite	finger	hand	self
gu	V	V	KCL		V	[MC]	N	PRO

ft   Having finished speaking, she bit her finger.

ref mosquito:47

tx	Hai	giọt	m u	vừa		chảy	ra,	n ng
mg	two	droplet	blood	just^now		flow	go^out	damsel
gu	NU	GC	N	AV		V	[V]	KCL

tx	liền		ngã		quy	xuống	đất	chết	v
mg	act^immediately		fall^down		collapse	go^down	earth	die	and
gu	[V]		V		V	V	N	V	CJ

tx	biến		th nh		con	muỗi.
mg	disappear		turn^into		animal	mosquito
gu	V		V		MC	N

ft   As two drops of blood flowed out, she immediately collapsed [to] the ground [and] died and turned into a mosquito.

ref mosquito:48

tx	Ch nh	vì		vậy	m	muỗi	luôn
mg	precisely	because^of		thus	that	mosquito	continuously
gu	AV	PRT		DM	REL	N	AV

tx	luôn		tìm	người	để	cắn	vì		nó	muốn
mg	continuously		seek	person	for	bite	because^of		3s^ARROG	want
gu	AV		V	GC	[PRE]	V	PRT		PRO	V

tx	lấy	lại	hai	giọt	m u	đã		mất	để
mg	get	again	two	droplet	blood	[toˆhaveˆalready]		lose	for
gu	V	[AV]	NU	GC	N	ASP		V	[PRE]

tx	được	trở	lại	kiếp	người.
mg	beˆableˆto	become	again	life	person
gu	ASP	V	[AV]	N	GC

ft [It is] precisely because of this that the mosquito incessantly seeks people to bite, because it wants to get back the two drops of blood [it] has lost in order to be able to come to life again.

References

Adams, Karen L. 1986. Numeral classifiers in Austroasiatic. In Colette Craig (ed.), Noun classes and categorization: Proceedings of a symposium on categorization and noun classification, 242–62. Philadelphia: John Benjamins Publishing.

———. 1989. Systems of numeral classification in the Mon-Khmer, Nicobarese and Aslian subfamilies of Austroasiatic. Pacific Linguistics, Department of Linguistics Research School of Pacific Studies. Canberra: The Australian National University.

———. 1991. The influence of non-Austroasiatic languages on numeral classification in Austroasiatic. Journal of the American Oriental Society 3(1):62–81.

———. 1992. A comparison of numeral classification of humans in Mon-Khmer. In Mon-Khmer studies 20:91–109.

——— and Nancy Faires Conklin. 1973. Toward a theory of natural classification. Papers from Ninth Regional Meeting Chicago Linguistic Society, April 13–15, 1973, ed. by C. Corum et al. Chicago, IL: Chicago Linguistic Society.

———, Alton L. Becker, and Nancy Faires Conklin. 1975. Savoring the differences among classifier systems. Papers from the 5th International Conference on Sino-Tibetan Languages and Linguistics, October, 1975, Berkeley.

Allan, K. 1977. Classifiers. Language 53:285–311.

Barker, Miriam A. 1995. [Personal communication]. Dallas, TX.

Becker, A. J. 1986. The figure a classifier makes: Describing a particular Burmese classifier. In Coletter Craig (ed.), Noun classes and categorization: Proceedings of a symposium on categorization and noun classification, 327–43. Philadelphia: John Benjamins Publishing.

Benedict, Paul K. 1975. Austro-Thai language and culture: With a glossary of roots. Cambridge, MA: Human Relations Area Files Press.

Cao Xuan Hao. 1988. The count/mass distinction in Vietnamese and the concept of 'classifier'. Zeitschrift für Phonetik, Sprachwissenschaft, und Kommunikationsforschung 1:38–47.

Chafe, Wallace, ed. 1980. The pear stories: Cognitive, cultural, and linguistic aspects of narrative production. Norwood, N.J.: Ablex.

Clancy, Patricia M. 1980. Referential choice in English and Japanese narrative discourse. In Wallace L. Chafe (ed.), The pear stories: Cognitive, cultural and linguistic aspects of narrative production, 127–202. Norwood, N.J.: Ablex Publishing Corporation.

Clark, Marybeth. 1992. Conjunction as topicalizer in Vietnamese. Mon Khmer Studies 20:91–109.

Comrie, Bernard. 1985. Languages of the world: Who speaks what. In N. E. Collinge (ed.), An encyclopedia of language, 956–82. New York: Routledge.

―――, ed. 1987. The world's major languages. London and Sydney: Croom Helm.

Craig, Colette, ed. 1986. Noun classes and categorization. Proceedings of a symposium on categorization and noun classification. Amsterdam: Johns Benjamins Publishing.

Craig, C. A. 1994. Classifier languages. Encyclopedia of Language and Linguistics 2:565–69. Oxford: Pergamon Press.

Crystal, David. 1992. An encyclopedic dictionary of language and languages. Cambridge, Mass.: Blackwell.

Cyr, Danielle. 1993. Crosslinguistic quantification: Definite articles vs. demonstratives. Language Sciences 15(3):195–[215].

Đặng Chấn Li u and L Khả Kế. 1989. Từ điển Việt-Anh. H Nội: Nh Xuất Bản Khoa Học Xã Hội. Hanoi: Social Sciences Publishing House.

DeLancey, Scott. 1987. Sino-Tibetan languages. In Bernard Comrie (ed.), The world's major languages, 787–810. London and Sydney: Croom Helm.

Denny, J. Peter. 1976. What are noun classifiers good for? In Salikoko S. Mufwene, Carol A. Walker, and Sanford B. Steever (eds.), Papers from the 12th Regional Meeting Chicago Linguistic Society, April 23–25, 1976, 122–32. Chicago: Chicago Linguistic Society.

References

———. 1986. The semantic role of noun classifiers. In Colette Craig (ed.), Noun classes and categorization: Proceedings of a symposium on categorization and noun classification, 297–308. Philadelphia: John Benjamins Publishing.

Dixon, R. M. W. 1986. Noun classes and noun classification. In Colette Craig (ed.), Noun classes and categorization: Proceedings of a symposium on categorization and noun classification, 105–12. Philadelphia: John Benjamins Publishing.

Downing, Pamela. 1986. The anaphoric use of classifiers in Japanese. In Colette Craig (ed.), Noun classes and categorization: Proceedings of a symposium on categorization and noun classification, 345–75. Philadelphia: John Benjamins Publishing.

Du Bois, John W. 1980. Beyond definiteness: The trace of identity in discourse. In Wallace Chafe (ed.), The pear stories: Cognitive, cultural, and linguistic aspects of narrative production, 203–74. Norwood, N.J.: Ablex Publishing Corporation.

Dyvik, Helge J. J. 1983. Categories and functions in Vietnamese classifier constructions. Norway: University of Bergen Dept. of Linguistics and Phonetics.

———. 1991. Classifiers and individuation. In Papers from the Twelfth Scandinavian Conference of Linguistics, 50–65. Reylijante: Linguistic Institute, University of Iceland.

Emeneau, M. B. 1951. Studies in Vietnamese (Annamese) grammar. Berkeley: University of California Press.

———. 1956. India as a linguistic area. Language 32:3–16.

Erbaugh, Mary S. 1986. Taking stock: The development of Chinese noun classifiers historically and in young children. In Colette Craig (ed.), Noun classes and categorization: Proceedings of a symposium on categorization and noun classification, 399–436. Philadelphia: John Benjamins Publishing.

Flexner, Stuart Berg and Leonore Crary Hauck, eds. 1987. The Random House dictionary of the English language. Second edition, unabridged. New York: Random House.

Fuller, Judith Wheaton. 1988. Topic and comment in Hmong. Bloomington: Indiana University Linguistics Club.

Gage, William W. and H. Merrill Jackson. 1953. Verb constructions in Vietnamese. South East Asia Program, Department of Far Eastern Studies. Ithaca, N.Y.: Cornell University.

Givón, Talmy. 1979. On understanding grammar. New York: Academic Press.

———. 1983. Topic continuity in discourse: An introduction. In Talmy Givón (ed.), Topic continuity in discourse: A quantitative cross-language study, 5–41. Philadelphia: John Benjamins Publishing.

———. 1984a. Syntax: A functional-typological introduction, vol. I. Philadelphia: John Benjamins Publishing.

———. 1984b. The pragmatics of referentiality. Paper presented at the Georgetown Round Table Conference on Languages and Linguistics, Washington, D.C.

———. 1990. Syntax: a functional-typological introduction, vol. II. Philadelphia: John Benjamins Publishing.

Goral, Donald R. 1978. Numeral classifier systems: A Southeast Asian cross-linguistic analysis. In Graham Thurgood, James A. Matisoff, and David Bradley (eds.), Linguistics of the Tibeto-Burman Area, 4.1, Fresno: California State University.

Greenberg, Joseph. 1977. Numeral classifiers and substantival number: Problems in the genesis of a linguistic type. In A. Makkai, V. B. Makkai, and L. Heilmann (eds.), Linguistics at the crossroads. Padova: Liviana Editrice, Lake Bluff: Jupiter Press.

Gregerson, Kenneth J. and Marilyn B. 1995. [Personal communication]. Dallas, TX.

Heimbach, Ernest E., comp. 1969. White Hmong-English dictionary. Linguistics Series 4, Data paper 75. Southeast Asia Program. Ithaca, N.Y.: Cornell University.

Hinds, John. 1983. Topic continuity in Japanese. In T. Givón (ed.), Topic continuity in discourse: A cross-linguistic study. Amsterdam: Johns Benjamins.

Honey, P. J. 1956. Word classes in Vietnamese. Bulletin of the Oriental and African Studies University of London 18(3):534–44.

Hopper, Paul J. 1986. Discourse functions of classifiers in Malay. In Colette Craig (ed.), Noun classes and categorization: Proceedings of a symposium on categorization and noun classification, 309–25. Philadelphia: John Benjamins Publishing.

Huffman, Franklin E. 1986. Bibliography and index of mainland Southeast Asian languages and linguistics. New Haven, Conn.: Yale University Press.

——— and Tran Trong Hai. 1980. Intermediate spoken Vietnamese. Ithaca, N.Y.: Southeast Asia Program, Cornell University.

Hữu Ngọc. 1995. Sketches for a portrait of Vietnamese culture. Hanoi: Thế Giới Publishers.

Huỳnh Đình Tế. 1990. Vietnamese language materials sourcebook. Folsom, Calif.: Southeast Asia Community Resource Center.

Jones, Robert B. and Huynh Sanh Thong. 1960. Introduction to spoken Vietnamese. Program in Oriental Languages B, 8. Washington, D.C.: American Council of Learned Societies.

Lehman, F. K. 1990. Outline of a formal syntax of numerical expressions, with especial reference to the phenomena of numeral classifiers. Linguistics of the Tibeto-Burman Area, 13(1):89–120.

Li, Charles N. and Sandra A. Thompson. 1981. Mandarin Chinese: A functional reference grammar. Berkeley: University of California Press.

Matisoff, James A. 1991. Areal and universal dimensions of grammatization in Lahu. In Elizabeth Closs Traugott and Bernd Heine (eds.), Approaches to grammaticalization, vol. 2, 383–453. Philadelphia: John Benjamins Publishing.

Nguy n Dang Li m. 1975. Cases, clauses and sentences in Vietnamese. In S. A. Wurm (ed.), Pacific Linguistics Series B, 37. Canberra: Department of Linguistics Research School of Pacific Studies, The Australian National University.

———. [1974–79]. A classification of verbs in Vietnamese and its pedagogical implications. In S. A. Wurm (ed.), Pacific Linguistics Series C(1):193–213. Canberra: Department of Linguistics Research School of Pacific Studies, The Australian National University.

———. 1969. Vietnamese grammar: A combined tagmemic and transformational approach. In S. A. Wurm (ed.), A contrastive analysis of English and Vietnamese. Pacific Linguistics Series C, 2. Canberra: The Australian National University.

Nguyễn Đinh Hoa. 1957. Classifiers in Vietnamese. Word: Journal of the Linguistic Circle of New York 1:124–52.

———. 1987. Vietnamese. In Bernard Comrie (ed.), The world's major languages, 777–96. London and Sydney: Croom Helm.

———. 1991. Vietnamese-English dictionary. Rutland, Vt.: Charles E. Tuttle Co.

Nguyễn Như Ý. 1994. Thư mục ngôn ngữ học Việt Nam: Tiếng Việt, Tiếng Anh, Tiếng Ph p, Tiếng Nga. H Nội: Nh Xuất Bản Văn Hóa. Bibliography of Vietnamese linguistics: Vietnamese, English, French, Russian. Hanoi: Nh Xuất Bản Văn Hóa.

Nguyen, Phuong and Loan Nguyen. 1994. [Personal communication]. Dallas, TX.

Панфилов, В.С. 1988. О В'етнамских классификаторах. Вопросы Языкознания, том 37, но. 4, 59–69. Москва.

Panfilov V. S. 1988. O V'etnamskikh klassifikatorakh. Voprosy Yazykoznaniya, tom 37, no. 4, 59–69. Moskva.

Purnell, Herbert C., Jr., ed. 1962. A brief description of the Miao language by Miao Language Team, Division of Minority Languages, Institute of Races, Chinese Academy of Sciences. In Miao and Yao linguistic studies: Selected articles in Chinese, translated by Chang Yü-hung and Chu Kwo-ray, 1–25. Linguistics Series 7, Data paper 88. Southeast Asia Program. Ithaca, N.Y.: Cornell University.

Ratcliff, Martha. 1991. Coverbs, the underspecified noun, and syntactic flexibility in Hmong. Journal of the American Oriental Society 3(1):694–703.

Riddle, Elizabeth M. 1989. White Hmong noun classifiers and referential salience. Paper presented at the XXII International Conference on Sino-Tibetan Languages and Linguistics. Manoa: University of Hawaii.

Shibatani, Masayoshi. 1991. Grammaticization of topic into subject. In Elizabeth Closs Traugott and Bernd Heine (eds.), Approaches to grammaticalization, vol. 2, 93–133. Philadelphia: John Benjamins Publishing.

Строганов, В.А. 1974. К идентификации классификаторов В'етнамского языка. Вопросы структура языка: синтаксис, типология, И.К. Лекомцев, 162–73. Москва: Наука.

Строганов, В.А. и И.И. Ревзин. 1974. Гипотеза о двучленности ядра группы существительных во В'етнамском языке. Вопросы структура языка: синтаксис, типология, И.К. Лекомцев, 140–52. Москва: Наука.

Thompson, Laurence C. 1965. Vietnamese reference grammar. In Stephen O'Harrow (ed.), Mon-Khmer Studies 13–14. University of Hawaii Press.

────── and Nguyen duc Hiep. 1961. A Vietnamese reader. University of Washington Press.

Thompson, Sandra A. and Hilary Chappell. 1991. The semantics and pragmatics of associative DE in Mandarin discourse. In Patricia M. Clancy and Sandra A. Thompson (eds.), Asian Discourse and Grammar. Santa Barbara Papers in Linguistics, vol. 3, 171–86. Santa Barbara: University of California Department of Linguistics.

Tran, Anh. 1994. [Personal communication]. Dallas, TX.

Trần Văn Điền and L Tinh Thông. 1992. Ng y xưa ở qu hương tôi: Mô'i tình ngưu lang v chức nữ, Once in Vietnam: The bridge of reunion and other stories. Lincolnwood, Ill.: National Textbook Company.

——— and Trần Cảnh Xuân. 1993. Ng y xưa ở qu hương tôi: Chiếc bóng tr n tường, Once in Vietnam: A shadow on the wall and other stories. Lincolnwood, Ill.: National Textbook Company.

T'sou, B. K. 1976. The structure of nominal classifier systems. In P. N. Jenner, L. C. Thompson, and S. Starosta (eds.), Austroasiatic studies 1215–47. Hawaii: Oceanic Linguistics Special Publication no. 13, Part II.

Tuan Duc Vuong and John Moore. 1994. Colloquial Vietnamese: A complete language course. New York: Routledge.

Wang Fu-shih. 1957. The classifier in the Wei Ning dialect of the Miao language in Kweichow. In Herbert C. Purnell, Jr. (ed.), Miao and Yao linguistic studies: Selected articles in Chinese, translated by Chang Yü-hung and Chu Kwo-ray, 111–185. Linguistics Series 7, Data paper 88. Southeast Asia Program. Ithaca, N.Y.: Cornell University.

www.ingramcontent.com/pod-product-compliance
Lightning Source LLC
Chambersburg PA
CBHW050139240426
43673CB00043B/1723